CURIOSITIES SERIES

Oklahoma
CURIOSITIES

QUIRKY CHARACTERS, ROADSIDE ODDITIES & OTHER OFFBEAT STUFF

PJ LASSEK

INSIDERS' GUIDE®

GUILFORD, CONNECTICUT

AN IMPRINT OF THE GLOBE PEQUOT PRESS

The prices, rates, and hours listed in this guidebook were confirmed at press time. We recommend, however, that you call establishments to obtain current information before traveling.

To buy books in quantity for corporate use or incentives, call **(800) 962–0973** or e-mail **premiums@GlobePequot.com.**

INSIDERS' GUIDE®

Text design: Nancy Freeborn
Layout: Debbie Nicolais
Maps: created by Rusty Nelson © Morris Book Publishing, LLC
Photo credits: p. 7 Courtesy Broken Arrow Chamber of Commerce; p. 22 Wollaroc Museum Bartlesville, OK; p. 54 Courtesy Denise Morris; p. 56 Courtesy of Poteau Chamber of Commerce; p. 119 Courtesy of POM Incorporated; p. 184 First Christian Church; p. 197 P_Bar Farms Maze/Loren Liebscher; p. 206 Photo © 2004 by Derek Arndt. Used with Permission; p. 214 Waurika Fire Department; p. 227 Kenton Museum Inc.; p. 230 *The Boise City News*/C.F. David; p. 251 Jim Powers Collection; and p. 254 Courtesy of Catina Duvall. All other photos courtesy of the author.

ISSN 1935-6463
ISBN 978-0-7627-4126-7

Printed in the United States of America
10 9 8 7 6 5 4 3 2 1

For my late mother who taught me the value of taking on challenges, my Polish father who taught me the importance of being able to laugh at myself, and to Ami, who is a shining light in my life.

OKLAHOMA

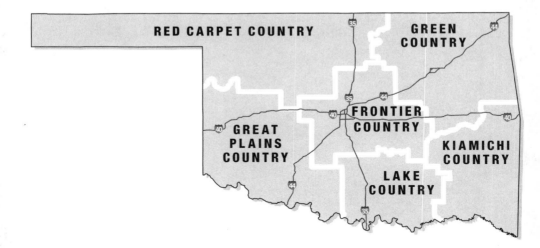

Contents

Acknowledgments

My heartfelt thanks goes out to all of the members of the numerous Chambers of Commerce, librarians, and town officials across the state who opened my eyes to places unknown to me and introduced me to a host of delightful Oklahomans. A special thanks goes to Melyn Johnson of Guymon and Jessika Davis of Duncan.

Introduction

To appreciate Oklahoma is to understand who she is. As noted in the song bearing her name, Oklahoma is the land "where the wind comes sweepin' down the plain" sometimes in excess of more than 200 miles per hour. But when you live in the heart of Tornado Alley, that's expected and because of that, it was chosen as the film site for a blockbuster movie about a twister.

Although Oklahoma twisters will throw a fair share of dust your way, Oklahoma has had its share of unfair ridicule by outsiders who have described it as being dust-filled and drab. But, those who have bothered to take the time to notice are well aware that the state has had a traumatic and tumultuous history; it is far from boring.

First things first: Oklahoma is not flat. There are flat parts, but it also has five mountain ranges, 24 percent of it is covered by forest, and it has more man-made lakes than any other state. Even though Oklahoma is one of the youngest states in the nation (it celebrated its one-hundredth birthday in November 2007), the findings unearthed beneath the Spiro Mounds date American Indian civilization here as far back as A.D. 850. There also are historical recordings that in 1541 Spanish Explorer Francisco Vásquez de Coronado trekked through the state on his quest to find the "Lost City of Gold." Skeletal remains of Jurassic proportion are but another finding in this state where the "June bugs zoom" and the "wavin' wheat sure smells sweet."

There's no doubt that Oklahomans have a sweet amount of self-pride in many ways. In recent years it appears they have taken little shame in the notion that the state abounds with rednecks. Now hold your horses before you criticize; it's all a matter of context here. Redneck in its kinder form is more popular than ever. Songs are written about rednecks from Gretchen Wilson's "Redneck Woman" to John Michael Montgomery's "Paint the Town Redneck." Some of the more popular southern comics whose whole repertoire is about rednecks play to sold-out audiences here, who embrace redneckism. Finding a redneck is so popular with tourists traveling Route 66 across Oklahoma that a couple from Erick have capitalized on it creating the Mediocre Music Makers, Annabelle and Harley, self-proclaimed rednecks, a two-person act that brings in hordes of visitors into the tiny eastern town. There is no denying that Okies do love their guns, gambling, pickup trucks, mobile homes, chewing tobacco, big hairdos, Sonic drive-ins, and Wal-Mart. In fact, anyone traveling the state will quickly realize that a town isn't a town if a Sonic or a Wal-Mart isn't spotted shortly after crossing the town limits.

The red in Oklahoma transcends the red in the dirt and red in the necks; Oklahoma is also a red state known for its staunch Christian conservatism that is very much alive with liquor stores barred from sales on Sunday, and up until 2006 tattoo parlors were outlawed. So when a 60-foot-tall monument depicting the prayerful hands of the state's most famous faith healing evangelist was erected, it only seemed fitting. After all, Oklahoma is part of the Bible Belt stronghold and often is referred to as the belt's buckle.

It seems like being the buckle of the Bible Belt is about as good of a directional location for Oklahoma as anything else. That characteristic is pretty clear. What's not so clear is whether the state fits in the South, Midwest, or Southwest. The natives here do talk slang but not necessarily with a drawl, and the state does sit below the Mason-Dixie. It also would be rare if you couldn't find a diner serving biscuits and gravy, chicken fried steak, okra, pinto beans, and cornbread, yet some of the most rural areas are home of vineyards producing fine wines. There is even one city within the Mountain Standard Time Zone.

Oklahoma is diverse. It is a place where farmers, ranchers, oil barons, roughnecks (not to be confused with rednecks), American Indians, and freedmen all took part in its evolution despite the political antics along the way. It seems like in most recent times when asked the question, Okies will say the state is located in America's Heartland, a name bestowed on it by outsiders during the media coverage of the 1995 Oklahoma City bombing.

Heart is one thing Okies do have. Through perseverance of the forced relocation of the American Indians, the hardships of the Dust Bowl and Great Depression era, the Race Riot of 1921, the oil bust of the mid 1980s, and the 1995 Oklahoma City Bombing, the one thing that has remained unbroken is Oklahoma's spirit and ability to rebound, while never losing a sense of the lighter side of life.

Journalist and author John Gunther said it best: "No state except possibly Oklahoma has a history so bursting with wackiness and furor."

Anyone who ventures into Oklahoma will no doubt come away with what Okies already know; in fact, it's stamped right on their license plates: Oklahoma is OK.

GREEN COUNTRY

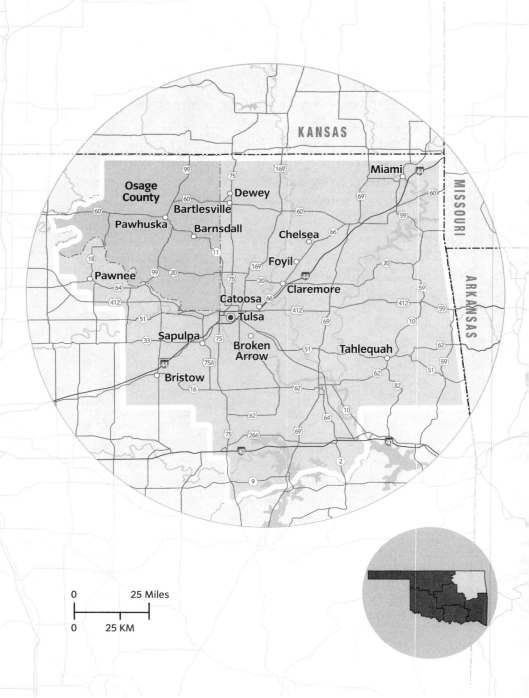

GREEN COUNTRY

Located in the northeastern part of Oklahoma, Green Country gets its name from the large amount of vibrant green foliage found in and around the area's mountain ranges, rolling hills, and tallgrass prairies. Green Country is home to the High Plains featuring the Tallgrass Prairie Preserve near Pawhuska where hundreds of buffalo freely roam. Getting more rain than the state's other areas, Green Country is the greenest, and wettest, part of Oklahoma. It also is home to more lakes than any other area of the state.

Green Country is also known for another liquid—oil. Tulsa, the second-largest city in the state, achieved the title Oil Capital of the World early in the twentieth century due to its large number of oil wells. Its oil reputation grew internationally.

Tulsa was originally named Tulsey Town by the Muscogee Creek Indians. The name is a variation of Tullahassee, meaning "old town." With the discovery of the black gold that lay beneath its surface, Green Country became home to rich oil barons in the early 1920s, and the oil riches paved the way for spectacular art deco skyscrapers in Tulsa, the only kind in the world influenced by the American Indian, and the only Frank Lloyd cantilevered skyscraper in Bartlesville. History later gave the name of Drillers to Tulsa's minor league baseball team. The image of the roughnecks who manned the oil rigs was also the inspiration for one of Tulsa's most well-known landmarks, the *Golden Driller,* a statue that towers over the city.

Green Country is headquarters for three of the largest Indian tribes in the state—the Muscogee Creek in Okmulgee, the Cherokee in Tahlequah, and the Osage in Pawhuska. All three now have large casinos operating in or near Tulsa. One Native American who rose to become Oklahoma's Native son was Will Rogers, who hailed from Oologah, situated almost in the dead center of Green Country. Rogers's ability to make serious points about life and politics with his Okie style of humor-reality, absent biting sarcasm, was a gift that captured audiences everywhere. He said that he never met a man he didn't like, and there's a lot to like about Green Country—both people and places.

Location, Location, Location
Barnsdall

Visitors are still drawn to this once-booming oil town, which could have all but dried up with the days of the 1980s oil bust had it not been because of the distinction bestowed on oil well No. 20. Drilled in 1914 by Indian Territory Illuminate Oil Company, the well initially sat on the outskirts of Bigheart, a small community named after Osage chief James Bigheart. It was one of four towns designated as government-established land for the Osage Nation.

Well No. 20 was only a feeder well, pumping about four to five barrels a day and was active up until several years ago, according to Bob Evans, publisher of the *Barnsdall Times* newspaper. It isn't the well itself that has continued to bring the town some unusual status, but its whereabouts. It's the world's only Main Street oil well.

During the 1920s when oil fever was rampant, this community's population began to explode. A few years later, the townsfolk decided to change the town's name from Bigheart to Barnsdall in an effort to capture some of the recognition from the nationally known Barnsdall Oil

Company, which operated two refineries in town. Later, the town acquired more land to its west and extended Main Street, which happened to stretch directly into the well. Because the well was in operation, officials decided that instead of rerouting the street, they would incorporate the well into the middle of it. That decision not only gained the well landmark status, even Ripley's Believe It or Not! acknowledges it as the world's only Main Street well.

The bust of the oil boom days put an end to the refineries and also caused the town's population to dwindle to less than half of what it was during its heyday. But, well No. 20 and its unusual location continue to pump interest for sightseeing travelers. The well sits on Main Street at the curve of Highway 11.

Well No. 20 is the world's only Main Street oil well.

Momma's Boy

Bartlesville

Men getting tattoos honoring their mothers is old hat, but Ron Jones has taken the artistry of tattooing dear old "Mother" to a new level. The fifty-eight-year-old salesman and deliverer of welding supplies admits he is obsessed and doesn't fully understand his fascination with inking himself, not once, not twice, but twenty-four times with etchings of the "Mother Road," otherwise known as Route 66. Around town he is easily spotted sporting a short-sleeved stonewashed denim shirt with a tailor-made rectangular hole across the shoulders that exposes his latest tribute to her.

The Bartlesville resident has spent the past fourteen years behind the silver-chained steering wheel of his classic red, white, and blue 1956 Chevy getting his kicks on Route 66. His wife, Roz, said she isn't sure whether the Chevy will ever travel beyond the white lines that frame the

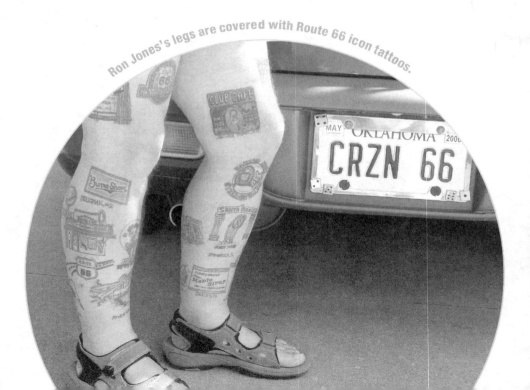

Ron Jones's legs are covered with Route 66 icon tattoos.

route from Chicago, Illinois, to Santa Monica, California. Their vacations are spent traveling different sections of the highway, revisiting the sites and meeting other Route 66 enthusiasts.

The first signs of Jones's tattoo interest appeared when he was fifty-one. It was a simple black-outlined design of the old Route 66 highway shield. By age fifty-six, Jones was inked with his twenty-fourth tattoo, the most conspicuous one of all. Positioned across his upper back, shoulder-to-shoulder, and in living color is an exact likeness of Cool Springs gas station, in Cool Springs, Arizona. This tattoo gained him a spot in the Cool Springs' Hall of Fame. Other tattoos cover his lower legs and arms. Anyone familiar with Route 66 will likely recognize at least one of the colorfully inked sites.

Jones said he doesn't have a favorite tattoo. They all represent meaningful memories of sites where he met other Route 66 travelers, from retirees to foreigners seeking to experience what is left of Americana. There are sites like the Snow Cap Drive-In in Seligman, Arizona, where the owner, Juan Delgadillo, used humorous antics to entertain his customers, such as spraying them with mustard-looking silly string. The sign on the door read SORRY WE'RE OPEN. Jones said news of Delgadillo's death in 2004 at the age of eighty-eight was taken hard by the Route 66 community of enthusiasts because he was a real character.

Jones gets a little defensive about any references to a midlife crisis gone awry and he jokes that he isn't brain damaged, even though he spent many of his more youthful years cracking stacks of cinderblock with his head until forced to quit. Jones says he thinks his obsession is really nothing more than a tribute.

"It's about preserving what is left of her through me. She's a part of me," Jones says.

When it comes to Route 66, Jones proudly admits, "I'm a momma's boy." If you don't catch a glimpse of Jones in town, you can e-mail him at tattoo66man@sbcglobal.net.

Self-inflicted Butt Shot
Bristow

In 2004 a twenty-seven-year-old Bristow resident, who armed himself during a manhunt of an escaped prisoner, ended up with a butt load of explaining to do when his efforts thwarted the police search.

The man decided, as a precaution in case the escapee showed up in his neighborhood, to load his .22-caliber pistol, cock the hammer, and stick the gun inside his belt just above his rump. But, when the man later tried to retrieve the pistol, it snagged on his clothing and fired a round into his left buttock. Realizing what he had done, he was able to walk to his parents' home nearby; they took him to the emergency room.

When police heard on their scanners that a shot was fired and a man was wounded, the manhunt for the escapee was interrupted while police investigated the shooting incident. But without crime or serious injury, the man was treated and released—and valuable time in the search for the real criminal was lost. To this day, the escaped prisoner has not been caught.

What's All the Crowing About?
Broken Arrow

Outsiders may find themselves crying fowl at Rooster Days, one of the oldest festivals in the state. The festival has nothing to do with roosters anymore, but this seemingly misnamed event doesn't appear to ruffle the feathers of its host city. In fact, Broken Arrow residents really don't give it a second thought. The town has been holding Rooster Days every May for more than seven decades. Old-timers say that just because roosters no longer play a role, it doesn't mean the name should change. After all, the name wasn't plucked out of thin air; there was a time when the roosters did rule.

It was in the early 1930s when this event was hatched as a way to cull excess cocks that were fouling efforts to create an infertile egg market in the hen houses. In those days refrigeration didn't exist yet and keeping dairy products fresh at the market and at home was a task in and of itself. You see, fertile eggs spoiled much faster, and farmers counted on their eggs because they were a commodity that held bartering power at local markets. The fresher the egg, the better the trade for farmers, who had families to feed and clothe.

A few businessmen decided to make an event out of their crusade to freshen the egg supply. They knew there was a market for roosters if they could collect at least two tons of them. So one day in May, the businessmen got farmers to clean out their chicken pens of excess roosters, and they bought all the roosters for a one-day-only bird purchase at premium prices. Farmers, their roosters, and townsfolk flocked in great numbers to Main Street for a day of rooster-related contests and prizes and the big sale.

Old Life magazine photo of Broken Arrow Rooster Days.

The event was a success and grew each year, evolving beyond the culling of roosters. Top talent, parades, the Miss Chick pageant, carnivals, contests, wrestling matches, and rodeos became an integral part of the event even as poultry farming waned. Today, the four-day event, held the second weekend in May, focuses mainly on entertainment but still includes the pageant and carnival. The only chicken to be found is deep-fried, and the only crowing to be heard is by the local chamber of commerce over the attendance of tens of thousands of people. For more about Rooster Days, contact the Broken Arrow Chamber of Commerce at (918) 251-1518.

Whale of a Tale

Catoosa

When Hugh Davis decided in the late 1960s to surprise his wife, Zelta, with a handmade gift on their wedding anniversary, little did he know the splash he would make.

A retired Tulsa zoo director, Davis built an 80-foot-long, concrete blue whale for their oversized pond, located just outside of Catoosa along historic Route 66. Davis chose to put the whale there to create a fun swimming hole for the entire family.

But it wasn't long before word of this wide-eyed, smiling marine mammal's presence circulated throughout town. Waves of people started showing up at the private swimming hole, wanting a chance to be swallowed up by the larger-than-life sea-dwelling novelty. The popularity of the blue whale drove Davis to open the swimming hole to the public. He hollowed out the whale's mouth so kids could be "swallowed up." Inside the mouth and belly of the whale is a slide that shoots out the side and a steel ladder that can be climbed to peek out portholes. A diving platform is perched on the tip of the whale's raised tail. Near the swimming hole Davis even installed heart-shaped concrete picnic tables mounted atop baby whales.

The swimming hole was a hub of activity every summer throughout the 1970s and most of the 1980s. Passing motorists, whose curiosity was piqued by the eye-catching cetacean, often stopped to check it out. Over time, happenings at the blue whale spawned a host of stories, like the time a lifeguard feared a corpse resided beneath the water after finding a set of human teeth on the bottom of the lake. The teeth

Jocie and Allison, their mother Paulette Reynolds, and their aunt Ami Reynolds spend a fall afternoon at the swimming hole.

were actually dentures that apparently belonged to a fellow who lost them while diving off the whale several years earlier. Mrs. Davis reportedly told the media about the teeth, and the man returned to claim his dentures. He told Mrs. Davis that he was too embarrassed at the time he lost them to ask for help in finding them.

To everyone's dismay, Mrs. Davis closed the water park in 1988 due to her husband's failing health, and the whale began to deteriorate. The death of Mr. Davis two years later was feared to be the harpoon that would end the life of the whale for good. But the growing popularity of sites along Route 66 in the early 1990s turned the weathered whale's future around. The peeling paint, murky water, overgrown foliage, and posted KEEP OUT signs didn't prevent Route 66 enthusiasts from seeking out the site.

Recognizing the significance of the blue whale and its spot along Route 66, the Catoosa Chamber of Commerce acquired grant money in 1995 to assist the family in restoring the whale, and the surrounding area. Unfortunately, swimming is no longer allowed. But when you hear about the blue whale that resides in a Green Country lake, it's no fish story.

The Blue Whale sits on the west side of Route 66 on the north side of Catoosa. You can't miss it.

Who Needs a Realtor When You Have a Sears Catalog
Chelsea

When it came time to buy a house, Joseph Sterling Hogue did what many American home buyers were starting to do in 1913: He picked up the Sears and Roebuck catalog and thumbed through the pages until he came to his dream home—Modern Home No. 146, the Saratoga.

In 1908 Sears and Roebuck revolutionized home buying by offering prefabricated houses in its catalog. The houses were shipped to buyers around the country, arriving with a lengthy set of assembly instructions and building materials carefully keyed to a set of blueprints. The modern homes featured the latest in residential technology. Of the nearly one hundred thousand catalog homes Sears sold between 1908 and 1940, it is believed that only one of them was built in Oklahoma—the Hogue house.

Unlike other homebuyers who ordered the houses from the catalog by mail, Joseph Sterling Hogue actually traveled to Sears and Roebuck in Chicago, Illinois, and laid down sixteen hundred dollars for The Saratoga and returned to Chelsea with it.

The two-story home with a partial wraparound porch is still standing in good condition in the small rural community of Chelsea, Oklahoma, along Route 66. It has eight rooms, four of which are bedrooms; one and one-half baths; and a basement. It also came equipped with electric lights, an amenity no other home in Chelsea had back then.

Up until her death in the summer of 2005, Hogue's daughter Erskine Stanberry lived in the house, which she strived to keep in its original form. In 1990 it was added to the National Register of Historic Places. Although Erskine did make some changes when it came to carpet, heat, and air-conditioning, many of the original features, such as the exterior siding, the ornate windows, the oak beams, the staircase, the bathtub, and the electrical fixtures, remain intact.

If Joseph Sterling Hogue were still alive, he might wonder why, with all the recent popularity surrounding do-it-yourself home improvements and reconstruction, there isn't a new market for prefabricated homes. The Hogue home (now occupied and loved by a new set of owners) is located at 1001 Olive Street. It is east of Route 66 on the southeast corner of Olive and Tenth Streets.

The Sears and Roebuck catalog home Joseph Hogue built in 1913, one of only a few that still remain.

Trigger Happy
Claremore

John Monroe Davis was seven years old when his father bribed him to take his medicine. The compensation was a Belgium muzzle-loading .410 shotgun. Young John ingested the unpleasant elixir, and that gun, which cost $1.50 at the time, triggered a lifelong love of firearms. Davis would eventually own one of the largest gun collections in the world. By the time John Davis died at age eighty-five in 1973, the former hotel manager and former Claremore mayor had built a collection of more than 20,000 guns, which are now housed in the J.M. Davis Arms and Historical Museum. Today his collection is valued at around $7 million.

Kind of a Flintlock Blunder-Buss, a rifle used in the 1700s.

Davis began displaying his gun collection around 1917 in the lobby of the now-razed Mason Hotel in downtown Claremore. Over the years he would collect the rarest of items, including a Kolibri "Hummingbird," the world's smallest manufactured automatic pistol, and an ancient Chinese hand-cannon more than five hundred years old. His collection also includes a set of guns wielded by notorious outlaws Pretty Boy Floyd, Jesse James, and Bonnie Parker.

It's reported that Davis acquired many of his guns through artful trade negotiations. This bargaining often occurred while he was working the night shift at the hotel he managed. By 1929 Davis had ninety-nine different types of firearms, and as his collection continued to grow, so did the display. Guns decorated the hotel's front desk, lined the walls, filled the windows, and engulfed seven of the hotel rooms.

In 1964 Davis made a deal with the state to lease out his collection for a dollar, and in return the state would build and maintain a museum. The museum opened in 1969, free to the public. Later, a 1840s-style gunsmith shop was added to the museum loaded with gunsmith tools from Pennsylvania and a workbench.

The J.M. Davis Arms and Historical Museum, which houses more than 20,000 guns, is located at 333 Lynn Riggs Boulevard. For more information call (918) 341-5707.

When Your Carry-on Carries You Home
Dewey

Preserved behind locked glass in a Dewey museum lies the killer of legendary Western star Tom Mix. The unusual display draws visitors from around the country, who gape in disbelief. Was Mix's death karma, or just eerie happenstance?

At age ten, Mix's life changed after attending one of Buffalo Bill's Wild West Shows. The Pennsylvania boy decided he wanted to be a show cowboy, and he began learning and perfecting his quick-draw and trick-riding skills. At age twenty-two, Mix headed to Oklahoma, where eventually his death-defying trick-riding ability and superb horsemanship got him discovered and swept off to Hollywood. From 1909 to 1935, he starred in 336 films, most of which were silent. He gained matinee idol status and earned $6 million. He was also the highest paid

Peggy Berryhill, manager of the Tom Mix Museum, poses in front of the two metal Halliburton suitcaes that killed Mix.

circus performer in history to exhibit trick-riding skills and overall horsemanship, earning a weekly salary of ten thousand dollars.

What many people may not know about Mix is how he spent his
early days before stardom. Shortly after coming to Oklahoma, Mix was
hired as a night marshal in Dewey (he had to make a living some way
and had several odd jobs before being discovered). He had an uncanny
ability to detect bootlegged liquor—a talent that landed him the
moniker, Pussyfoot Mix. He was known to walk the train cars and town
establishments, eradicating stashes of illegal booze. He would kick suitcases and shove crates with his foot, listening for a particular-sounding
slosh.

"Its gurgling warble is unmistakable," Mix said about the sound of
liquor.

Mix spent several years terrorizing suitcases and jolting trunks in his
successful detections of illicit alcohol. So how odd is it, really, that a
metal Halliburton suitcase would deliver the fatal blow to Mix? It was
1940, and Mix, a well-established western star, was cruising in his 1937
yellow convertible Cord 812 Supercharged Phaeton on Highway 89
between Tucson and Florence when he unexpectedly approached a
detour, swerved off the road, and abruptly came to a stop in a dry
riverbed. The force of the sudden stop hurled his metal suitcase forward from the backseat hitting Mix on the back of the head, cracking
his neck, and instantly killing him.

Investigators looked into the unusual death of one of Hollywood's
more popular celebrities. It wasn't really a hard case to crack, but more
of a crack from a hard case.

Mix's suitcase and other belongings are in the Tom Mix Museum in
Dewey at 721 North Delaware. A thirty-seat theater plays Mix movies.
For more information call (918) 534-1555.

What a Lovely Fiddleback! Violin, That Is.
Foyil

Over his lifetime Ed Galloway, who could make anything out of nothing, masterfully carved three hundred violins, an obsession that had nothing to do with music and everything to do with wood. The fiddles, you see, were just a means to showcase his collection of exotic woods that he obtained while stationed in the Philippines during the Spanish-American War.

Galloway's love for woodcarving began at an early age while he was growing up in Missouri, and it was rekindled after he returned from the war in 1904. In preparation for the 1915 Panama-Pacific Exposition, Galloway carved a number of different elaborate scenes in scraps of wood that he displayed in a Springfield, Missouri, shop. A major fire in the shop, however, destroyed all his carvings except a large walnut piece that he had carved with serpents and reptiles. On his way to the exposition in San Francisco, Galloway and the walnut piece got as far as Tulsa

Violins hand-carved by Ed Galloway can be found in the Fiddle House.

before his money ran out, and they didn't make it to the exposition. His luck, however, didn't run out altogether. Galloway landed a job as a woodworking teacher at the Sand Springs Home orphanage in Sand Springs, Oklahoma, after the home's founder Charles Page came across the walnut carving temporarily displayed at a local drugstore.

It wasn't until after Galloway retired and moved with his wife to rural Foyil, Oklahoma, that she coaxed him into building a house to display all of his instruments and all of his woodcarvings. They called the structure the Fiddle House. Each of Galloway's fiddles is unique, some with carvings on the fiddle's scroll, others with inlaid patterns of exotic woods. He didn't own fancy tools; in fact, he often used pieces of broken glass to hollow out the instrument's body or to create a certain cut. Galloway is said to have been inspired by his musical brother to carve violins as a way to display his exotic wood. Over the years, people fed his hobby by sending him wood from around the world. In 1962, after Galloway died, nearly two hundred of the three hundred fiddles were stolen from the Fiddle House, and they were never recovered. The dwindled collection, however, still draws hordes of admiring visitors.

The Fiddle House is located at Totem Pole Park on Oklahoma 28A about 4 miles east of Route 66 in Foyil. It is open to the public year-round. For more information call (918) 342-9149.

NINETY-FOOT FOYIL FETISH

Ed Galloway was a master woodcarver. He realized this creative interest as a youngster, but it wasn't only uniquely carved fiddles he left in his legacy. It wasn't until he retired in 1937 that he began his quest to sculpt the largest totem pole in the world as a tribute to the American Indian. It was this brightly colored, 90-foot-tall, 28-ton, steel-reinforced concrete sculpture that elevated Galloway to folk-artist status. There doesn't appear to be a totem pole like Galloway's anywhere else in the world.

Galloway, whose formal education stopped at eighth grade, had little experience with masonry, but that didn't stop him—a vision is a vision. So, with bucket after bucket of cement and rocks, Galloway began an eleven-year effort to construct his vision of a totem pole that features two hundred different carved images. At the top are four Indian figurines. Sitting Bull of the Sioux faces north; a Comanche chief faces south; Apache Geronimo looks to the west; and Chief Joseph of the Nez Perce looks to the east.

The totem pole was placed on the National Register of Historic Places in 1999. Galloway never wanted fame; all he reportedly wanted was to pay homage to the American Indian. The sculpture is located in Totem Pole Park on Oklahoma 28A about 4 miles east of Route 66. Public access is free.

Ed Galloway constructed a folk-art totem pole of concrete.

We'll Leave the Light On for You

Miami

There are many ghost stories floating around Oklahoma, but none like the one about the Spook Light that hovers over the countryside northeast of Miami. The light appears suddenly, displays eerie movements, and then disappears quickly into the darkness. The mysterious illumination mostly performs its nocturnal dance near the Quapaw reservation during the July powwow. There's no denying the Spook Light's existence, for too many have seen it. Even the U.S. Corps of Engineers in 1946 failed to find a scientific explanation for the brightness that bounces about. The first recorded sighting dates back to 1886. However, it is reported that the Quapaws spotted the light long before then.

The theories behind the Spook Light are plenty, ranging from area legends to unproven scientific explanations. One of the oldest tales comes from the Quapaws and involves love, greed, and sacrifice. A young Indian brave and maiden are forced to elope when the maiden's father demands a dowry the brave cannot pay. When the lovers hear that warriors were sent to find them, they commit suicide by leaping off a cliff into Spring River. It is believed the light represents the spirit of the lovers.

Another story is about an old miner crossing the fields at night with his lantern, who never makes it home. It is said the light is the old man's lantern bobbing along the highway.

The Spook Light has been investigated by many, including science students and military personnel, who hoped to uncover the answer behind the phenomenon. In 1955 a group of students spent a weekend investigating it. They arrived with every type of photographic, electronic, and communication device in existence at that time and examined mine gases, car light reflections off of nearby Highway 66, and atmospheric electricity—all to no avail.

The Quapaws, however, warn that the light should be left alone for spirits should not be taunted.

The stretch of road a few miles long that is called Spook Light Road by the locals is located on county road E50 a few miles south of Miami between Interstate 44 and the Missouri border. You will very likely get accurate directions if you stop and ask where it is.

The site has even been featured on National Public Radio during a Halloween special—a reporter claimed to have even seen the light.

Don't Go Losing Your Head
Osage County

Out of all the museums in Oklahoma, Woolaroc is perhaps the one most people leave shaking their noggins in disbelief. While nearly all the museums in the state, including Woolaroc, evolved from oilmen's Wild West collections, none have a display that makes eyes pop and jaws drop like the exhibit of the South American shrunken heads. "Eeewww! Are they for real?"

According to the curator nobody can absolutely verify that the heads are of Jivaroan tribe members shrunken into "tsantsas," a good luck symbol that contains magical powers and protects the possessor of any spiritual revenge from the beheaded. But six of the seven heads have been scientifically determined to have the characteristics of true tsantsas. The seventh head, that of a small child, is thought to be a counterfeit.

Tsantsas were in great demand by the white man after infiltrating the Jivaro region in the 1850s. The founder of Woolaroc, oilman Frank Phillips, was given the heads in the 1930s—three from his son and the others from a friend.

The heads are a very small part of the Woolaroc experience. The museum is nestled in the Osage hills between Barnsdall and Bartlesville on a fourteen-thousand-acre compound, most of which contains a wildlife preserve for buffalo. The area was the 1924 site of Phillips's ranch home, Woolaroc, named after the landscape of woods, lakes, and rocks.

In 1929 Phillips turned his airplane hangar on the ranch into the museum. One of the first displays was his small, single-engine monoplane that won a 1927 race from Oakland, California, to Honolulu, Hawaii, just five months after Charles Lindbergh's famous flight. The museum also displays a range of Phillips's belongings such as ancient Indian artifacts found in an Oklahoma archaeological dig and a collec-

Shrunken heads displayed at Woolaroc.

tion of Colt firearms. It also has a section of outlaw memorabilia. Once a year, Phillips would hold the Cow Thieves and Outlaws Reunion. Western celebrities, lawmen, and local outlaws would attend the party. Woolaroc was designated as a neutral zone, so at the end of the night, the outlaws were given a thirty-minute head start before they were considered fair game again.

Although Woolaroc's curator likes to downplay the popularity of the shrunken heads by pointing out all the priceless paintings, sculptures, and artifacts on display, it's those heads that seem to, well, stick in your head. Oh, did I forget to mention the human-finger necklace? Woolaroc is located on Highway 123 about 6 miles north of Barnsdall and 12 miles south of Bartlesville. Call (888) 966-5276 for hours or visit www.woolaroc.org.

Ghostbusters
Pawhuska

Only in the buckle of the Bible Belt can you bust any notion of paranormal activity by simply voting that it is not so. After all, the majority rules, doesn't it? Well it did with a majority of the Board of Trustees of Pawhuska's Constantine Theater, who in 2005 quashed its chamber of commerce's attempt to capitalize on the longstanding lore that surly spirits haunt the 1880s playhouse.

The theater was originally built in 1880 as the Pawhuska Hotel before C. C. Constantine purchased it in 1911 and turned it into a theater. It's believed to be haunted by Constantine's daughter, Sappho, and other rowdier prairie spirits. In recent times, during building restoration projects, workmen repeatedly reported hearing footsteps and seeing an apparition of a girl. Other witnesses tell of hearing long bouts of noise that sounded like barroom brawling.

The chamber's proposal for the theater was innocent enough and merely an economic development scheme: The plan would create tours of the theater based on the lore to draw those mortals eerily curious about spirit-world activity. It would be a town attraction and give needed exposure to the underutilized facility, which holds only one to two community shows a year.

But some of the theater trustees got spooked when the Paranormal Investigation Team of Tulsa wanted to bring in its high-tech night vision and audiotape equipment, along with its thermometers and hygrometers to examine and document the unexplained occurrences. A fracas ensued among the trustees over whether to allow the plan to go forward. There were references to scripture and advice from preachers. In the end, the majority said they refused to be "second-line prostitutes to Satan" by allowing the devil to secure a place in Pawhuska through sanctioned paranormal activity.

Director Dia Doughty stands outside the Constantine Theater.

GREEN COUNTRY

Chamber director Dia Doughty said the trustee president told her that the ghoulish plan was a dead issue because the board took a vote and the majority decided that "we don't have ghosts."

"That's when I asked if the board of trustees would vote me skinny and rich," Doughty quipped.

So instead of stamping out the ghostly belief, the conflict among the trustees actually strengthens the lore that the brawling prairie spirits often leave those who have entered the theater somewhat irritable. The theater, listed on the National Register of Historical Places, is located at 100 West Main Street. Call the Pawhuska Chamber of Commerce at (918) 287-1208 for information about events.

That Stink Just Won't Go Away
Pawhuska

Pawhuskans never paid that much attention to Osage Indian John Stink and his pack of dogs until the day he reappeared from the dead. As anyone might expect, that feat not only raised some eyebrows, but also downright scared some and caused others to keep a closer eye on this man of simple means.

Born in 1863, Stink refused to accept the encroachment of the white man's culture. He lived outdoors as his ancestors did, creating a great divide between him and civilization. His wealth as an oil-royalty beneficiary played little to no role in his life. He would appear in town adorned with his signature head wear, a scarf or kerchief wrapped around his head and tied beneath his chin; an Indian blanket draped diagonally across his torso; and either a cigar or pipe in his mouth. He often sat in front of the mercantile and fed his stray dogs large amounts of steak—the dogs thought the wealth was delicious.

Then one day Stink was found unconscious. After failed attempts by

25

a medicine man to revive him, he was declared dead and buried in the Osage fashion—above ground in a semi-reclining position and covered with rocks. But a few days later, Stink was spotted roaming the streets of Pawhuska with his pack of dogs. The story of his resurrection spread like wildfire. Astonished, many Osages believed Stink had returned as a ghost. Apparently, the Osages, spooked by this feat, shunned him. Now it is suspected that instead of actually dying, Stink likely suffered from a malady like diabetes and went into a diabetic coma only to later regain consciousness and climb out of his rock sepulcher. Some townsfolk thought he suffered from alcoholism and say that when he was found "dead" a second time in a snow drift frozen stiff and was again buried, he was really just in a drunken stupor because he later reappeared and returned to his hermit life. It's unclear whether these were two separate incidents, or just different versions of one incident. Eventually, a cabin was built for the aging Stink a few years before he died in 1938, but Stink rarely spent time inside it.

Stink's cabin still stands today, and when he did actually die he was buried in the city mausoleum. For more information on the legend of Stink, visit the Osage Nation Tribal Museum at 819 Grandview Street or call (918) 287-5441.

John Stink sitting on a tree stump on his land.

POPULATION STATS

American Indians make up 8 percent of Oklahoma's residents. The state has the second-largest population of American Indians in the nation. Tulsa has the second-largest population of American Indians among the nation's cities. Oklahoma City ranks fourth. Many of the estimated 250,000 Indians living in the state are descendants from sixty-seven tribes that inhabited Indian Territory. There are thirty-nine tribal headquarters located in Oklahoma.

Crimestopper

Pawnee

One of the nation's most notorious murder-kidnappings occurred gangster style in the small community of Pawnee in 1931, when two local thugs from the Big Boy Caprice gang gunned down the owner of the town delicatessen during a robbery and took the owner's beautiful daughter, Tess Trueheart, hostage. For months, newspapers across the nation published a daily account of how Trueheart's fiancé, a hard-nosed, plainclothes detective, led a dragnet that nabbed the crooks and rescued her. This high-profile case was the beginning of a long and successful crime-fighting career for Dick Tracy.

Chester Gould, creator of the world famous square-jawed, trench-coated, fedora-topped detective, was raised in Pawnee. He moved outside of Chicago as a young adult, where he pursued his comic strip career bringing to life a heroic lawman during the revered heyday of mobsters like Al Capone.

It was through Dick Tracy's battles with evil that Gould unveiled to the world grotesque villains whose names foretold their moral turpitude. Among those embedded in the minds of Americans are Flattop Jones, Breathless Mahoney, Larceny Lu, Chameleon, Boris Arson, Pruneface, and the Mole. Many of Gould's characters and settings were based on real people and places from his childhood and hometown. For instance, Tracy's first story was set in Pawnee, and the delicatessen is based on the old Fischer Bakery. Gould's character, Brilliant, who invented Tracy's most famous two-way wrist radio, was patterned after Pawnee resident, Otis Porter, who once built a radio out of old Model-T parts. Gould's scruffy character, B. O. Plenty, was modeled after Pawnee local, Billy Whiskers. Gould also featured the names of ten of his high school classmates on businesses throughout the three-panel cityscape in his September 25, 1946, strip.

Gould spent much of his adult life in Woodstock, Illinois, which led to an embarrassing moment on *Jeopardy,* when the show listed Woodstock, instead of Pawnee, as his birthplace. Gould never forgot his Oklahoma roots, and Oklahomans haven't forgotten him. Every year, on the second Saturday in October many of the nearly two thousand Pawnee residents come to the courthouse square to celebrate Dick Tracy Day. The featured attraction is a mile-long parade of law enforcement vehicles from agencies across the state. So for one day out of the year, Pawnee has enough cops to hold criminals at bay. I'm sure Dick Tracy sees it as a day of opportunity for crooks to run havoc elsewhere. An extensive Dick Tracy exhibit is housed at the Pawnee County Historical Society, located at 513 Sixth Street. For more information call (918) 762-4681.

Gladys Kitchen holds a card Chester Gould created for her father, Otis Parker, who inspired Gould's character Brilliant.

WHAT WERE THE ODDS?

American Indians becoming big players in economic prosperity was a long shot that has had huge payoffs for tribes who have ventured into casino gaming.

Green Country is home to many tribes, including the Five Civilized Tribes—Cherokee, Chickasaw, Choctaw, Muscogee Creek, and Seminole—who were forced to Indian Territory in the 1830s.

In April 2006, the tribes celebrated the one hundredth anniversary of the Five Civilized Tribes Act of 1906, in which the federal government recognized tribal governments. This act laid the groundwork for how tribes would regenerate in future years, and regenerate they did. A few days after the anniversary celebration, it was reported that Oklahoma had more than eighty Indian-run casinos, exceeding the neighboring states of Kansas, Missouri, Arkansas, and Texas, which had a combined total of about thirty gaming sites. The Chickasaw have the largest casino in the state near Norman that is nearly double the size of Las Vegas' Caesar's Palace.

The Cherokees have the next largest gaming industries in the state with its major casino located in Catoosa. The Muscogee Creeks are expanding their casino in Tulsa to rival the size of the Cherokees, and the Osage Indians have opened casinos in Tulsa and in Sand Springs.

When Oklahoma's elected officials were creating gaming compacts with the tribes, they intended for the state to benefit significantly from the profits. Instead, the revenue to the state is significantly less than predicted, an outcome that has received political criticism. It appears that this time, the hand the government dealt the tribes has paid off in the tens of millions for the tribes, much of which goes to support tribal social programs and education along with economic development endeavors.

GREEN COUNTRY

What You Can't Fit in the Car, Stick in the Trunk
Pawnee

A thirty-two-year-old Pawnee woman found herself bagged by the criminal-justice system in 2003 after a trip to a Wal-Mart. She was stopped by police, arrested, and charged with felony child endangerment in Payne County District Court.

When the woman left the store, she was seen putting children in the trunk of her Honda Accord. Witnesses called police. Officers found the woman's two daughters, ages nine and ten, snug in the trunk. Apparently, there was no room for the woman's purchases and all of her passengers. There was another adult in the front seat and five other children, ages one to fifteen, in the back seat. The woman said she put the center armrest of the back seat down to provide air to the trunk. The woman later plead guilty to the charges.

Don't Bite the Hand That Arrests You
Sapulpa

In 2003 a thirty-six-year-old Sapulpa man was sentenced to life in prison for biting and then spitting on a police officer, who had answered a domestic disturbance complaint at the man's residence in a local trailer park. Although medical testing over nine months indicated that neither the man nor the officer had any communicable diseases, the jury reached its verdict in fifteen minutes. The man's attorney told the judge at sentencing that the man was remorseful for his drunken behavior. The judge rejected the defense's plea for a lesser sentence. Instead, he imposed the life sentence, plus one year for resisting arrest and domestic abuse. The man had a criminal past.

Send in the Clown

Sapulpa

In 2005 a thirty-seven-year-old Sapulpa man was jailed for contempt in municipal court after appearing dressed as a cop clown on the day of his traffic case. The man had painted his face white, the area around his eyes black, and his mouth red, and he was wearing a red ball on his nose. He was sporting a police uniform shirt, a toy badge, and a Keystone Kops helmet over a curly, bright-blue wig.

The man refused to alter his appearance despite warnings from police and the judge. One officer reportedly said that "Bozo" apparently had a problem with authority. Besides contempt, the man was charged with refusing to identify himself to police as he was booked into jail. The man was reportedly sent for a mental evaluation not long after he was jailed.

Put the Pedal to the Metal

Sapulpa

It is said that the difference between men and boys is the size of their toys. Well, that may not ring true for Terry Smith, a retired mechanic, who has a driving passion for cars—toy pedal cars. He has quite a collection, thirty or so cars that he built by hand. He also has tons of smaller metal toy cars, trucks, and buses, some of which he made, others he purchased. His garage has been renovated into a showroom that displays the collection. It's more than impressive to the adult. Who knows what a child would think?

"I don't know, I must have been deprived of toys as a boy," Smith said shrugging shoulders.

Smith is fascinated with cars of any make and year as long as they are metal with pedals.

Smith is unassuming about his talent, referring to the incredible cars as "just stuff." The obsession started in 1982. He always had a passion for the press steel toy trucks that were made in the 1920s. Smith said he began by buying new cars and then selling them. Then he moved to buying old cars, restoring them, then selling them. Before he knew it, he was building a reproduction of a car. He says it's just a hobby that keeps him off the road and out of trouble.

Terry Smith and some of his favorite pedal cars.

"The bottom line is that I simply can't afford to buy the ones I really like, so if I want it I have to either build it, or don't have one," he said.

A little Stutz was his first car and then a Skippy Fire Chief was his second, and the passion grew from there. Smith said his favorite cars are his yellow 1930 Jaguar and his 1956 pink and black Ford. The 1937 Lincoln and 1938 Sharknose Graham also come to mind.

Smith doesn't protect his collection. Over the years, his children were allowed to play with the cars. Now it's his grandchildren who pedal around. When Smith needs space, he says, he'll sell some of the cars and start building more. He said friends and family aren't so impressed with his hobby because they're used to it.

"It can be overwhelming when they first walk in, but after awhile nobody pays much attention to it," he said.

Smith said he doesn't see himself putting the brakes on his collection creations anytime soon. "I've got a lot of inventory to build. Where's the list? It's rattling around in my brain."

To get a peek at Smith's collection, call him at (918) 224-2451.

GREEN COUNTRY

The Mane Event
Tahlequah

On the outskirts of the college town of Tahlequah simmers a Hollywood scandal buried beneath an unassuming mound in a pasture off Highway 82 just past Moody's Curve. It is a twenty-six-year-old gravesite that has existed over the years with nearly no fanfare. Nobody knows if that is because it sits on private land or because of fears that too much attention might again raise questions about whether an imposter lies there.

For the locals who know about this gravesite, there is no identity crisis. They attest that the celebrity resting there is Mister Ed, the talented palomino, who mesmerized a generation of television viewers with his cynical words of wisdom. After all, there's a 5-foot tall headstone to prove it and no concrete evidence to dispute it. Some locals testify they visited the TV star during his retirement as he roamed the 17 acres north of Tahlequah.

In the late 1960s, horse trainer Clarence Tharp brought the palomino believed to be Bamboo Harvester, the real Mister Ed, to Oklahoma from California. Tharp even distributed cards advertising Mister Ed's availability for special events and invited youngsters to his farm to watch the equine perform his famous tricks. Tharp supposedly bought Bamboo Harvester for fifteen hundred dollars at an auction in 1966 after the CBS sitcom ended. He and the horse then retired to Tahlequah, where Mister Ed died in 1979 and was quietly buried in the pasture with a small wooden grave marker. When Tharp died, the land was sold, and the new owner didn't even know the grave existed until a neighbor mentioned it.

A decade passed before the scandal surfaced as a result of the media coverage of Tahlequah's first and only "Edstock." The fundraising event, sponsored by a Tulsa radio station, drew a crowd of two hundred from around the region to pay homage to the star. A granite

tombstone that reads HERE LIES MISTER ED was erected, and event atten-
dees sang songs and reminisced about their favorite episodes. Soon
after the event, the radio station received reports from Hollywood that
the famous horse died ten years earlier than the one buried in Tahlequah while living with his Oklahoma trainer Lester Hilton. Apparently,
the horse's death was never revealed to the press because the series
was starting to air in reruns. Although the show's franchise ordered the
Tahlequah grave promotion to cease, it could
not actually confirm that the horse
buried in Tahlequah isn't Mister
Ed.

Seth, Chloe, and Kaleigh show off the tombstone of Mr. Ed, which sits in their family's backyard.

If only Mister Ed were alive today, perhaps he'd have something humorous to say, because we all know that a horse is a horse, of course of course that is, of course, unless the horse is the famous Mister Ed. For more information call the Tahlequah Chamber of Commerce at (918) 456-3742.

Golden Boy
Tulsa

His confident stance, chiseled bare chest, and community presence, which rises above the city's landscape, has made him the talk of Tulsa for forty years. For some, he's an icon, and to others, he's a tacky eyesore. But everybody agrees the 76-foot-tall Golden Driller monument is an emblem of a bygone era, when oil gushed from Oklahoma's soil like a severed artery.

Perhaps to know him is to love this misunderstood, often-cussed local hero. He represents the brawn behind the brains in the petroleum industry. He is the roughneck who, soiled in crude oil, performed the dangerous job of building derricks and working drilling rigs in search of black gold. It was the success of the oil extraction that gave way to Tulsa's longtime moniker, Oil Capital of the World.

The original Golden Driller, in the form of papier-mâché, was first showcased in Tulsa at the International Petroleum Exposition in the 1950s. Sixteen years later, the Golden Driller, built of fiberglass, concrete, and reinforced steel, came to Tulsa permanently. His popularity with oilmen, not his artistic value, led to his spot in front of the QuikTrip Center, formerly called the IPE Building at the Tulsa County fairgrounds, once the home of the exposition. He is featured with a real oil derrick from a Seminole oilfield. He sports only gloves, a hard hat, dungarees, and work boots.

Over the years, this roughneck faced creative criticism and controversy. The first bout came when the company that built the statue put
its logo on a giant belt buckle despite orders stating that no corporate
insignia could appear on his hard hat (but the buckle isn't a hard hat,
now is it?). There also was an effort to clothe his bare chest, which was
deemed by some as too risqué for public viewing. Oilmen, however,
successfully argued that shirtless roughnecks were common during the
blistering summer heat. Today, he remains shirtless, but a makeover in
1979 altered the buckle to read TULSA. A few years back, the public also
foiled a proposal by the Fair Board to relocate him to the interior of the
fairgrounds, which would have placed him out of the sight of motorists.
Not all of the citizens thought the move was a bad idea.

The Golden Driller stands 76 feet tall and is located at the Tulsa County fairgrounds.

Not only has this state-designated monument and one of the most photographed subjects in Tulsa proven he can withstand 200-mph winds, but that he can also weather years of verbal assaults and a banishment attempt. So while most of the oil wells have stopped producing, the Golden Driller continues to stand tall. Rough around the edges and undignified, yet still golden. The statue is located on the north side of Twenty-First Street at Pittsburg Avenue.

Drink, Anyone?
Tulsa

Lurking in midtown Tulsa, are a villain, a hero, and a cast of characters spewing the message of temperance in a dramatic manner.

This group can be found every Saturday night in Tulsa Spotlight Theater's presentation of *The Drunkard,* a good old-fashioned campy melodrama. For more than fifty years, local actors have performed this temperance play every Saturday night to lively crowds in a cabaret-style setting, where the audience is expected to loudly root for the hero and to sling boos and hisses at the villain.

The theater is located in one of Tulsa's historic 1920s art deco homes, which was custom-built to include a recital hall on the insistence of the original owner, a piano teacher. In 1941 New York City actor Richard Mansfield Dickinson purchased the home. It was about ten years later that he and a group of actors sitting around his living room came up with the idea of forming a theater.

In 1953 the troupe gave its first performance, a condensed version of the 1890s melodrama, *Ten Nights in a Barroom,* that they divided into three acts and named *The Drunkard.* Although the tone of the original play was quite serious, depicting the moral dissolution, misery, and ailing conditions caused by drinking and particularly drunkenness, the

Spotlighters have delivered the message with humor and lots of slap-stick over the years.

It's truly an evening of old-fashioned fun sprinkled with sing-alongs even before the play starts and continuing throughout each of the three intermissions. Who can resist singing the likes of "Sweet Adeline," "Baby Face," and "My Wild Irish Rose," to name only a few of the fifty or so songs available in the program and sung accompanied by a piano. The evening is always topped off with a vaudeville act called *The Olio*, which includes performers of all ages.

The audience is offered free pretzels and the option to buy soft drinks, bottled water, and even an evil alcoholic beverage during the play. Between the play and the half-hour-long vaudeville act, the audience is also offered lots of free coffee and cookies. The curtain rises every Saturday at 7:45 p.m. at the theater located at 1381 South River-side Drive. For more information call (918) 587-5030.

A toast to vaudeville.

Reaching for the Sky

Tulsa

Tulsa is second in size to Oklahoma City, but it reigns when it comes to skyscrapers. Of the state's ten tallest buildings, Tulsa has six of them including the first top four.

The tallest in the state is Tulsa's Bank of Oklahoma Tower, coming in at 667 feet, or 203.3 meters. Then comes Tulsa's CityPlex Tower at 648 feet, or 197.5 meters, even though it has more floors than the bank tower. Skyscrapers, however, are not measured by floors because of different ceiling heights. Instead, they are measured by meters.

The third and fourth tallest in the state are Tulsa's First Place Tower at 516 feet, or 157.2 meters and the Mid-Continent Tower at 513 feet, or 156.3 meters. Oklahoma City's tallest building, Chase Tower, ranks fifth in the state at 500 feet, or 152.4 meters.

Tulsa's other skyscrapers that are included in the top ten tallest buildings in the state include Bank of America Center and the 320

The Bank of Oklahoma tower, right, is the largest skyscraper in the state.

South Boston Building coming in at ninth and tenth places. Oklahoma City has four in the top ten. In addition to the Chase Tower, there is the First National Center, City Place, and the Oklahoma Tower ranking sixth through eighth.

No Coffee for Me, Thank You

Tulsa

Irritate your wife and you may find that the freshly brewed cup of java she's handing you is your last—literally.

On November 29, 1954, forty-nine-year-old Nannie Doss made head-lines in Tulsa after admitting that she poisoned to death four of her five husbands over the prior ten years.

"I guess I shouldn't have had that second cup of coffee," her fourth husband and Okmulgee native Richard Morton was quoted saying about his lingering upset stomach. The forty-six-year-old man died the next day, May 19, 1953. Authorities later learned that the coffee con-tained enough liquid rat poisoning to kill twenty men.

Nannie's fifth husband, fifty-eight-year-old Tulsan Samuel Doss met his maker October 10, 1954, after drinking a cup of coffee. But his death didn't go unnoticed. Doss had been hospitalized before due to rat poison. After Doss died, his physician insisted on an autopsy, the results of which led to Nannie's arrest. According to her confession, it was Samuel's comment that "Christian women don't need a television or romance magazines to be happy," which sealed his fate.

This congenial, always smiling, and even sometimes giggling grand-mother told Tulsa authorities the triggers for her decisions to terminate her husbands ranged from teaching them a lesson to escaping her boredom. She was quoted as saying she killed her Tulsa husband because he simply "got on my nerves over little things."

Granted, her obsession with romance magazines and her search for the love of her life through lonely-hearts clubs left her selections somewhat shy of the perfect guy. Besides Doss and Morton, Nannie said she also poisoned her second husband, Frank Harrelson of Jacksonville, Alabama, who died in 1945 of rat poison mixed in a jar of his corn liquor, and her third husband, Arlie Lanning of Lexington, North Carolina, who died in 1952 of rat poison mixed in food and coffee.

Nannie's first husband, Charley Braggs, somehow survived without incident, but not without fear, which he reported was the ultimate reason he filed for divorce. Evidently, his fear was not without cause, since eight other of her relatives mysteriously succumbed to death under Nannie's care. It could be said that being related to Nannie Doss could be hazardous to your health.

To'errific

Tulsa

Since age thirteen, Betty Bell has been perfecting her God-given talent of whistling a clear rendition of nearly any tune requested. Now, in her mid-50s, the Tulsa Realtor can still give a foot-stomping performance for any crowd. She's not just any whistler. Instead of using only her lips, she is assisted not by two fingers, but by two toes. Betty is a nationally recognized toe whistler.

Betty attributes her toe-whistling feat to her cousin, who lived on a dairy farm in Kansas and was always whistling for the cows.

"She would stick her fingers way in her mouth and blare out a whistle," Betty said "I tried and tried and practiced and practiced and couldn't do it."

Betty said her realization that she could whistle with her toes happened by accident. "I always have been limber and I was sitting with my legs crossed trying to whistle. My classmate was over and she was teasing me and told me that I should try to do it with my toes because they looked like little fingers."

Betty said when she stuck her second and third toes into her mouth and blew, to her surprise it worked.

"We laughed and laughed until we almost cried," she said.

From then on, she said it was, "Hey, guess what Betty can do? Show 'em Betty."

Betty Bell whistles a tune while at River Parks near downtown.

Of course, she did and has been showing crowds locally, nationally, and even internationally for some time.

She has whistled for retirement parties, nursing home residents, local talent shows, charity events, and office parties. She went on two cruise trips, and yes, she whistled. It never fails, she said, no matter where she goes, once someone hears that she can whistle with her toes, she's begged to perform.

"People can't believe I can do it. They just have to see it," she said. "I get a real hoot out of watching people's reaction."

She said the older she gets the more interested people are.

"She can do what at her age?" Betty said people will ask.

Betty said she can only whistle with her right foot; she's tried with her left and it just doesn't work.

Betty made her national television debut in 1991 on *America's Funniest People*. Then in 2006, Bell made it on the Stupid Human Tricks segment of *The Late Show with David Letterman*. In December 2006, she appeared on *Good Morning America* and was given the *Missy Award*, dedicated to odd news that may have been missed during the respective year. Her appearance on *Letterman* also led to an invitation to Hollywood, California, to be on the game show, *I've Got a Secret*. Betty considers herself a professional since she got paid to whistle on *Letterman* and *I've got a Secret*. She also receives royalties each time the *Letterman* show airs her segment. She's gotten one check already. Betty said every once in awhile she gets recognized, or when people learn who she is, they say they saw her on TV. Betty said when her parents were living "they thought it was the greatest thing that I could whistle with my toes. My grandkids love it. When I returned from New York City, one of the kids said, 'Nanna, we saw you on TV with your toes.'"

What? You Can't Hear That?

Tulsa

There's a spot on the apex of a refurbished 1930s bridge in downtown Tulsa that for years had scientists scratching their heads and clearing their ears. It's an acoustical anomaly, a mystical phenomenon that Tulsa calls the Center of the Universe. There's no confirmed explanation as to why it does what it does; it just does.

Standing only on the concrete circle, thirty inches in diameter and encircled by fifteen rings of redbrick eight feet in diameter, one hears what those outside the spot cannot. While facing any direction and talking in a regular voice, the speaker sounds normal to someone within earshot. But to the speaker, the sound is strangely distorted. It's like talking into a synthesizer. The voice is amplified with a hollow metallic tone.

There is no signpost designating its location, and no admission fee to experience its oddity. It's a spot inadvertently integrated into what is now an urban-landscaped pedestrian bridge on Boston Avenue, connecting First and Archer Streets. In 1983 this once heavily traveled bridge over the railroad tracks that provided access to the old train depot was closed to vehicular traffic and reopened as a pedestrian pathway. The architect in charge of the conversion intended his redbrick circular design to be a metaphor linking the north and south sides of town. But, more people spend time in the middle of the bridge listening to their distorted voices than using it to traverse over the tracks.

Adding to the mystique of the bridge is a symbolic 60-foot, iron abstract totem-pole-like sculpture called *Artificial Cloud,* designed by American Indian artist Robert Haozous. It sits several yards to the south of the circle. Easy access to each of the sites is off Archer Street at the corner of Boston Avenue. For more information contact Downtown Tulsa Unlimited at (918) 583-2617.

Alicia Reynolds, left, can't hear her sister Megan's voice distorted at the Center of the Universe.

ORAL ROBERTS UNIVERSITY

Educating the whole man

d Jesus increased in wisdom and stature, and in favor with God and

The praying hands at Oral Roberts University.

Sleight of Hand

Tulsa

Believers and skeptics alike applaud the popularity of the proclaimed healing hands of televangelist Oral Roberts. They flock to see a statue of his hands protruding from the earth, larger-than-life and prayerfully posed at the entrance to the university that carries his name. The appreciation, however, is as different as the doctrine that separates the believers and the skeptics. Followers believe that God has used this Oklahoman's hands to heal through faith what the medical community cannot. Critics, however, contend Oral's healing sessions were nothing more than superb showmanship efforts to gain more believers. Either way, the 60-foot-tall bronze sculpture, which immortalizes Oral's revival-preaching, faith-healing journey, is one of Tulsa's most visited attractions.

The hands sculpture was originally erected in 1980 in front of the now-defunct City of Faith Hospital, which was built by the generosities of believers financially backing Oral's public announcement of his directive from God. When the hospital closed in 1991, the hands were relocated to the entrance of the successful Oral Roberts University. It is common belief that the giant bronze hands are an actual replica of Oral's hands because the artist used his sketch of the preacher's hands to create the small model that was viewed by officials. But the truth is the praying hands are not a replica of Oral's. Instead, the hands were modeled after Gary Mitchell's, the sculptor's neighbor. Apparently, the artist surmised that when enlarged to the enormous-sized sculpture, his neighbor's hands were more believable as the healing hands of the famous televangelist. The hands are located on the east side of Lewis Avenue north of 81st Street at the university's entrance.

No Stopping Him

Tulsa

An unyielding desire to reduce traffic accidents at uncontrolled inter-sections drove Tulsa police officer Clinton Riggs to design the first yield sign. Its keystone shape and yellow background with black lettering that read YIELD RIGHT OF WAY was slow to take hold, but once it did, it quickly became adopted as a traffic control measure worldwide.

In 1939 Riggs brought up his idea for the sign during a class discussion at the Northwestern University Institute of Safety in Chicago, and most of his fellow lawmen didn't think it would work. Most of them thought that using a yield sign for controlling traffic was far-fetched because it gave motorists too much trust to self regulate. The National Safety Council didn't give it much consideration either.

Tom Riggs shows off the first yield sign.

It wasn't until after World War II, when Riggs returned from service and was working as a Tulsa police captain of traffic control, that he decided to raise the issue of his yield sign again. This time, he got a better reception from fellow officers and worked with the city's traffic engineer to have two signs made up to experiment with on a trial basis.

When the mayor heard of this plan, he nixed it fearing that the city's liability had not been carefully examined. But despite the mayor and against the advice of the city attorney, Riggs proceeded with his plan, and in 1950 he erected the first yield sign at First Street and Columbia Avenue. He then parked a block away to watch the motorists' reaction. After motorists drove through the intersection, Riggs stopped the drivers to survey whether they understood the sign and, of course, they did.

When Riggs's experiment received positive publicity from the local press, the mayor flipped his position and took credit for what he called an "administrative decision." Dozens of signs were made and installed around the city.

Riggs received letters from around the country and from abroad about using his new traffic control sign. The United Nations decided to accept it as an international sign. In 1989 the Smithsonian received a sign from one of the first batches still in use in Derby, Kansas, and put it on display in the museum's transportation exhibit.

Riggs's son Tom has the first original sign hanging in his Oklahoma lake home. "Back then, you couldn't patent a safety device, so this was dad's free gift to humanity."

While the yield sign has evolved, changing from yellow to red and white bearing only the word, YIELD, its presence still brings traffic to a stop.

KIAMICHI COUNTRY

Spiro
McCurtain
Poteau
Heavener
Talihina
Big Cedar
Honobia
ARKANSAS
Antlers
Hugo
Swink
Millerton
Broken Bow
TEXAS

0   50 Miles

0   50 KM

KIAMICHI COUNTRY

If you are looking for the natural splendor of majestic mountains, crystal clear rivers, and abundant wildlife, you need look no further than Kiamichi Country in southeastern Oklahoma. Along with the wind-swept plains prevalent in the western part of the state, Oklahoma boasts four mountain ranges, two of which are in Kiamichi Country—the Kiamichis and the Oauchitas, a word that comes from the Choctaw meaning big hunt, testifying to the abundant wild life in the area.

If the wild that you're looking for is not something you spot in binoculars or the crosshairs of a hunting rifle, Kiamichi Country still has something to offer you. Nothing is more wild and exotic than the circus, and Kiamichi Country is the winter home of more circuses than any other place in the nation; not only did many past circus performers call Hugo their winter home, but many also chose the small southern town as their eternal home in the Showmen's Rest section of Mount Olivet cemetery.

Another point of interest is the wild, untamed mountainous flora in the Sans Bois Mountains (Wilburton) that hid outlaws like Belle Starr and Jesse James—aptly called Robbers Cave State Park. There also are locals who swear to sightings of Big Foot, drawing national attention to the dense forest region surrounding Honobia. If hiking through the forest to the top of a mountain is not in your reach, how about trekking up a hill? The world's tallest hill, Cavanal Hill in Poteau, gives beautiful views of the area around it.

Whatever type of wildlife you might be seeking, Kiamichi Country has something for you.

Goofy Golf
Antlers

In the first part of October, the Antlers Springs Golf Course holds the Spooky Goofy Golf Tournament, drawing some daring hackers onto a 9-hole course where clubs aren't really needed.

Tee shots are blasted out of cannons and propelled from slingshots. Some shots are made by players standing in toilets. The participants also use baseball bats, brooms, and cue sticks to advance their golf balls onto the green and into the hole.

The first round begins at 4 p.m., and a second round comes after nightfall, where glowing balls, hole flags, and the moon—if it's out—are the only things lit.

This toilet tee box is featured every year in October at the Spooky Goofy Golf Tournament.

The tournament used to be held near Halloween, but it was just too cold, said Butch Morris, owner and manager of the course. So, the tournament was moved up to the first weekend in October.

Morris said his wife entered one of the pictures she took of the event into the county fair and won a prize. The photo depicts a golfer standing in the toilet getting ready to tee off and the caption says: "Don't laugh, the pro said it would work."

Morris said the tournament is open to anyone bold enough to take on the challenges the game brings. Actually, after playing this tournament, Morris said the golfers seem to appreciate their own game of golf. For more information on the tournament date and entry fee, call Morris at (580) 298-9900.

When the Road to Prosperity Falls Flat

Big Cedar

Big Cedar appears to be nothing but a crossroads of two highways in southeastern Oklahoma. But on October 29, 1961, it drew tens of thousands of people when then-president John F. Kennedy dedicated the completion of U.S. Highway 259, which he pledged would change the economic face of the area.

All that is left of that historic moment for Oklahomans is a flagpole that constantly flies the U.S. flag and a small brass plaque at the pole's base. Without the large brown tourism sign identifying the president's dedication, the site would likely go completely unnoticed. Luckily the Poteau Chamber of Commerce still has the text of Kennedy's Big Cedar address, where he speaks of the future needs the country will have in the year 2000 and of the responsibility to ensure citizens still have the same great natural resources available to them.

US 259, a southern continuation of U.S. Highway 59 at Highway 63, is a shortened link through the Ouachita National Forest on Kiamichi Mountain that cuts 70 miles off the route of US 59, which stretches from Canada to Mexico.

Kennedy noted that opening access to the natural resources of eastern Oklahoma was the key to economic prosperity in the area. The logging companies have prospered, but at the crossroads called Big Cedar, there is only a tiny country store. When a store patron is asked if the store is all there is, he points across the street to the flagpole and says: "No. We have that."

The patron also points out a granite tombstone-style monument that he said was added a decade or so ago honoring Kennedy's life. While the flagpole sits in the open easement along US 259, the granite monument is tucked several yards to the west framed by tall shrubs and trees along Highway 63.

PRESIDENT
JOHN F. KENNEDY
DEDICATED US-259
OCTOBER 29. 1961

The memorial at the site where John F. Kennedy dedicated the completion of US 259.

Three Sticks into the Wind

Big Cedar

Around one of the numerous hairpin turns that make up a portion of U.S. Highway 259 as it stretches across Kiamichi Mountain is a site that certainly sticks out. It's a rock structure with three large red poles of varying heights protruding from its top about 20 feet into the sky. At first glance, it's obviously not a cell tower, a common sight along the mountain range. Instead, it's Three Sticks Monument. Its unusual design is definitely a vehicle stopper, and if that doesn't do it, the awesome view of the valley below and the neighboring mountain range will.

Three Sticks Monument is a symbol of the three precious resources of southeastern Oklahoma—land, wood, and water. It's a monument that actually honors five former politicians who were either primarily responsible for the completion of the highway that cuts through the

It's hard to miss Three Sticks Monument.

untamed mountain wilderness or were involved in promoting how the highway would enhance both recreation and economic opportunities in the area, which hasn't really happened.

The highway does shorten the southern route from Poteau to Broken Bow by traveling over the range instead of around it. But more importantly to some, it gives access to the marvels of the Ouachita National Forest and to the forest timber harvested by logging companies. Yep, it's those natural resources that are so valued.

Monumental Gesture

Broken Bow

The huge rustic wooden sculpture of a regal American Indian bust is not just another piece of commissioned art for the Forest Heritage Museum at Beaver's Bend Resort State Park north of Broken Bow. Instead, the Trail of Tears bust was a gift by Hungarian artist Peter Toth. This isn't just a guy from Hungary who decided to get some fame by gifting a sculpture that he couldn't sell. It does, however, beg the question as to why a guy from Hungary would not only gift a bust to a place in Oklahoma, but create a series and gift a different Indian bust to each of the other forty-nine states.

The Trail of Tears bust is part of Toth's fifty-state series called the Whispering Giants. It took Toth nearly twenty years to complete the series of busts he calls totem poles. Each is made out of large tree trunks. His mission started in 1971 and his statues are displayed at Indian reservations, welcome centers, museums, and parks. Toth, now living in Florida, says he donated these giant sculptures across the country to spread a humanitarian message he hopes will "soften our hearts."

To understand Toth's deed, you have to understand his life. He was born in Hungary in 1947, one of eleven children whose family lived a peasant farming life. At a young age, Toth experienced the wrath of Communist injustices on his family and others during the bloody 1956 uprising of the Russian military. Toth and his family lived in refugee camps throughout Europe for two years before his family was able to flee to America.

Trail of Tears totem pole carved by Hungarian artist Peter Toth at Beaver's Bend Resort State Park.

While being educated in Ohio, Toth was drawn to the stories of the American Indian when "the whiteman" discovered the new country. Many of the stories were all too familiar to those of his own family and countrymen. He said these statues are symbols of American Indian pride, and he wants to remind everyone of the proud race that inhabited America well before the arrival of Europeans.

Toth received no monetary compensation for his labor. He was, however, occasionally assisted with some living expenses as well as materials by cities, parks, and chambers of commerce.

The Oklahoma Trail of Tears totem pole can be seen year-round at Beaver's Bend Resort State Park located 7 miles north of Broken Bow off US 259. For more information call the Forest Heritage Center at (580) 494-6497.

Written in Stone

Heavener

Norsemen in Oklahoma? Fat chance, most Okies would say. This is America's heartland, home to the American Indian, not the Vikings. Those who insist it's unlikely obviously haven't traveled to Heavener in southeastern Oklahoma, because clearly the writing is on the wall on this one—literally. Hidden within the vegetation on Poteau Mountain in Leflore County is a huge vertical slab of stone more than 12 feet tall and 10 feet wide called the Heavener Runestone.

It is reported that a Choctaw hunting party in the 1830s first discovered the mysterious inscriptions carved into the mossy face of the hard sandstone slab that stands like a billboard in a 100-foot-deep ravine. However, it wasn't until the 1920s that a local, who had found the vertical slab a decade earlier, sent a copy of the symbols to the Smithsonian Institution and it determined the characters were runic. That triggered a quest by several people to find who penned the inscription. The endeavor was mainly led by Oklahoman Gloria Farley, who as a child had been shown the stone. It was Farley who named the slab the Heavener Runestone. Her theory is that Vikings sailed south along the Atlantic coast into the Gulf of Mexico and up the Mississippi before stopping and making their way on land to Poteau Mountain. It was Farley's undying enthusiasm over the stone that resulted in the creation of Heavener Runestone State Park, which was dedicated in 1970. The stone remains at its original site, but it is now encased in Plexiglass and covered by a wooden structure.

Heavener Runestone etchings are evidence that Vikings were in Oklahoma.

Through the decades of research there has been disagreement over what the symbols say. One expert says it is the date November 11, 1012, which coincides with a Norse settlement on the east coast in 1008. Another expert says it reads GLOME DAL, a land claim stating the valley is owned by GLOME. This expert dates the inscription to A.D. 600. The one thing all the experts agree upon is that the Vikings were on the northeast coast of North America one thousand years ago.

Thank goodness humans seem to have a need to profess their existence, record events, declare devotion, and mark their claims in a manner that is hopefully everlasting. Otherwise, it's doubtful anyone would have believed that the Vikings made their way to Heavener, Oklahoma.

The Heavener Runestone State Park is open year-round from dawn to dusk.

Giant Footprints
Honobia

The legend of Bigfoot, a 10-foot-tall, hairy, manlike creature, is alive and thriving in the forest of the Kiamichi Mountains. Now whether the actual beast exists is up for debate with most people, but not with those who live in Honobia, a small community nestled in the heart of 130,000 acres of mountain timberland and home to the only Bigfoot Festival in the state.

Despite the numerous unbending claims of Sasquatch sightings by local woodsmen, the physical proof just seems to fall short of materializing—no blood samples, no bones, no dead critter. What there is plenty of, however, are tales of chilling encounters often backed up with plaster castings of five-toed footprints 15 inches long and 7 inches wide, or pictures so blurry all that is depicted are blotches of earth-tone hues or a shadowy figure walking through a dense wooded area.

An unknown man (or is it?) provides excitement at the Bigfoot Festival in Honobia.

Although the Bigfoot lore in these parts dates back to when the Choctaw tribe dominated in the region, the sightings didn't really capture the ears of the outside world until 2000 when word got out that a local Honobia resident claimed he wounded a Kiamichi Yeti. The assertion caused the media to rain down on this town of 170 people, showering it with national attention unlike it had ever had before, and stories of encounters began to flood out of the mouths of locals. The Bigfoot Field Researchers Organization, which maintains a national database, has actually logged over sixty sightings in the state since 1971. Most outsiders scoff and snicker at those who insist the legendary Bigfoot exists because they have seen it, smelled it, or heard it crying out in the darkened forest.

The campy press coverage that played into the skepticism was heavily criticized by locals, who said the reports were aimed at embarrassing people instead of educating the world about a forest so vast and uninhabited that such a community of species could exist virtually undetected by scientists.

Town leaders saw the press coverage differently—it was an opportunity for the town to capitalize on the lore. In 2005 the first annual Bigfoot Festival was held the first weekend in October. The quaint event features two costumed creatures roaming around the rural fair-like festival. Belief in the beast or not, the highlight of the event is the storytelling session along the Little River, where hordes of people gather to hear the recounting of heartfelt testimonials once again. Call (580) 244-3992 for festival information.

Tall Tales from True Believers

Honobia

The story that introduced this small forest community of Honobia to the outside world came from woodsman Tim Humphreys in 2000, when he publicly claimed he had wounded a Bigfoot who had been terrorizing his family at their mountain home. At first the beast was just howling in the night. Then the creature began stealing venison from the outbuilding freezer. It was the boldness of the Yeti tapping on the house windows and finally rattling the doorknobs that caused Humphreys to confront it armed with a rifle. Humphreys recounted to investigators that when he stepped outside, he saw the beast charging toward him from a distance, and he shot it. The creature let out an eerie wail and retreated into the darkness. The

A common street sign found in the Kiamichi forest near Honobia.

next morning Humphreys said there was blood splattered on trees 9 feet high and for more than 150 yards. Humphreys also said a logger, who had been on the road that night, told him he saw two other Bigfoots carrying an injured creature along the highway. Of course, investigators failed to find the logger or any traces of blood that supposedly was washed away by a thunderstorm.

Humphreys' story is reminiscent of others, like the one told by an unidentified elderly man who said his grandfather actually killed the menacing Sasquatch. Convinced he had murdered a very large recluse mountain man, he buried the body and never spoke about it until many decades later.

"If only grandpa had told us where he buried it, we would have proof," the man told a crowd of eager believers.

There also is the dramatically told story of the bear hunters whose hound dogs went wild over a scent, racing deep into the woods well ahead of the hunters. Rustling of foliage, loud grunts, growling, and fierce barking ensued until a large cracking sound occurred, throwing the dogs into high-pitched yowling and yelping and causing them to retreat and later leading their owners to their find. But all that was there were enormous five-toed imprints in the softened earth. Photographs were taken to prove their find, said the hunter whose storytelling ability had captivated a crowd.

The hunter said he wished he had the photographs to show. But one night he had returned home to find there had been an intruder. On his table was the photo album opened to the very page displaying the footprints, and mysteriously they were gone.

Under God's Big Top
Hugo

Cemeteries are not places that people, including children, are usually eager to visit unless you're headed to Mount Olivet Cemetery in Hugo. In a special section of the cemetery called Showmen's Rest, you will find circus ringmasters, elephant trainers, trapeze artists, and other performers laid to rest in true circus style. This group of talented departed souls has traded their colorful costumes for equally creative tombstones that range from the vertical granite marker etched with a life-size drawing of Ringmaster John Strong in full circus regalia with top hat and tails to Jack B. Moore's much smaller gravestone carved into a replica of a Big-Top tent where he once featured bear wrestling acts. It

The Showmen's Rest section of the Mount Olivet Cemetery where circus entertainers are buried.

only seems fitting for Hugo to have a circus cemetery since the small southeastern town has been the winter home for a number of circuses since at least the early 1930s. In 2002 even the state declared the town Circus City USA because of its circus history. Hugo is now the winter headquarters to only two circuses—the Kelly Miller Bros. Circus and its sister circus, the five-ring Carson & Barnes, founded by Miller's brother, D. R., who is responsible for Showmen's Rest in the cemetery. D. R. purchased all the plots in the special section of the cemetery after Kelly died in 1961. According to one of the cemetery monuments, his goal was to create a tribute for the hardworking, talented circus performers.

Showman's Rest, located in a rectangular area marked by granite posts topped with elephants, is a magnet for visitors. That's understandable, the cemetery caretaker said, because you can learn a lot about the performers from their imaginative headstones. Take Zefta Loyal, for example, whose marker not only has her photo, but lets you know her talent—Queen of the Bareback Riders. During her heyday, she was billed as the only girl in the world that could perform somersaults over banners and hoops while riding bareback on a galloping horse, according to the Circus Fans Association of America. Then there is Ted Svertesky, an elephant trainer with Ringling Bros. and Barnum & Bailey Circus, who died at age forty in a circus-train wreck in 1994. Samuel Perez is another to die young. He was only thirty-two. A dynamic acrobatic and trapeze performer with the Kelly Miller Bros. Circus, Perez suddenly succumbed to an illness. In addition to the interesting gravestones are the amusing epitaphs, like Ted Bowman's etched on his circus wagon-wheel monument. It reads: "Nothing Left But Empty Popcorn Sacks and Wagon Tracks." Or, Donnie and Ione McIntosh, circus concessionaires, who remind everyone, "We have had the good life, but the season ended." D. R. Miller's epitaph may have himself "Dun Rovin," but his effort to provide an everlasting mark for circus folks sure has inspired a lot of roving in Mount Olivet Cemetery's Showmen's Rest.

The cemetery is located off Eighth Street on the south side of town. For more information call (580) 326-9263.

The Last Hole Just Killed Me
McCurtain

When you arrive at the front doors of Pine Acres golf course, hey, you made it, according to the hand-painted sign that hangs over the doors. The makeshift clubhouse/storage shed fronts a flat field on high ground near the water tower of this tiny rural town in southeastern Oklahoma.

There's something about the place that begs you to stop and inspect, especially if you are an inquisitive golfer—or a sightseer, for that matter. Initially, it's hard to tell whether someone is having fun with signs, or whether it's a real golf course. A peek into the clubhouse through the glass panes of the doors shows a row of golf club irons and balls on one side and a hodgepodge of flea-market-type stuff piled on the other.

The owner, Bob Wise, a seventy-six-year-old widower, is quite inviting, especially to the out-of-towner nosing around. He hawks the one-day special—free green fees—an offer too good for any golf hack to refuse. Otherwise, the hand-painted sign states it's four dollars for one game and twelve dollars to play all day on the homemade 10-hole, instead of the typical 9-hole, par 3 course.

There is no distinguishing between the fairways, rough, or greens. It's a pasture, and the tee boxes are marked with wooden surveyor stakes, and the holes are created with PVC pipe inserted flush into the ground. Two small plastic flags and several lollipop-shaped driveway reflectors indicate hole locations. Although putting is truly a crapshoot, Wise reassures trimming the grass around the cups at each hole with a 6-inch pair of silver scissors he pulls from his back pocket will make the

Bob Wise, owner of Pine Acres, stands ready to challenge anyone to his 10-hole golf course located on his pasture.

difference. It doesn't, but the trouble Wise takes to do it brings a little humor to the game.

There is never a quiet moment with Wise, who is full of stories, many of which are hard to believe. The topper centered around the deaths of his wife, daughter, and one of his sons. He tells how he had to bury them all too young. He boasts about the cedar coffins he kept making for himself, which he ended up using for them. The story gets interrupted when a ball is hit into a small pond. The tale gets picked back up as we head for the next makeshift tee box. There on the other side of a sparse vegetable garden and behind a small barn is the tee box but it is hard not to notice the nearby monument noting GRACE CEMETERY, and three commercial tombstones. Yep, buried right there in the middle of the golf course are his wife, daughter, and son, gravestones and all.

"I don't think it's legal to bury them here, but I wanted them close by," he said.

He sure sounded like he was spinning yarn. But at the end of the round, he insisted on showing off his last finished project. There tucked in a back room in his home lies a human-size rectangular cedar box. He smiles as he lifts the viewing lid of what he says is the fourth custom coffin he built for himself. The lid is lined inside with black velvet.

"I told my son that when I die just throw me in it and bury me out there next to mom."

There are some unusual golf courses around this state, but this just killed me.

You'll find this golf course just west of the water tower, which is visible no matter where you are in the tiny town of McCurtain.

Folklore That's Barking up the Wrong Tree
Millerton

Ask anyone in McCurtain County about the Wheelock Mission and Academy located in Millerton and their voices change. They don't mention that it's a National Historic Landmark or an important part of the Choctaw history that marks the tribe's forced immigration to Oklahoma in the 1830s, known as the Trail of Tears. Nor do they say it was an institution dedicated to education and Christian faith producing many Choctaw women who would later play significant roles in the tribal nation. Instead, their eyes widen and their voices take on this serious yet apprehensive tone.

"You know the Wheelock Mission is haunted, don't you?" an Idabel woman said when she was asked about it. "The trees, they bleed once a year, mourning those poor little girls. They were brutally murdered there a long, long time ago. I haven't actually seen the bleeding, but I've heard plenty about it."

Reverend Alfred Wright founded the Wheelock Mission in 1833. Six years later, he established the Wheelock boarding school for Choctaw girls on the same site as the mission. In 1884 the Choctaws built the academy, after a fire destroyed nearly all of the original campus. When the academy closed in1955, the campus had grown to seventeen structures, but by the late 1970s due to years of neglect and occasional fires, only seven abandoned structures remained.

Most area residents only seem to know about the folklore surrounding the longtime abandoned facilities. The legend's countless versions focus on the deaths of a few girls that occurred at the alleged hands of an intruder or from abusive beatings as school punishment, or in an unexplained fire. All the versions incorporate how some of the trees on the lawn bleed once a year, mourning the untimely deaths of the girls.

KIAMICHI COUNTRY

When you visit the academy, you'll find a row of mature trees near the main hall and many of the trees are visibly stained with dark marks that travel down the trunks like tears on a cheek. Other versions claim organ music, screams, and cries can be heard in the night, along with visions of unexplained candlelight and ghostly figures of the girls dancing. The stories of weird occurrences go on and on. Whatever the story, the girls are said to be secretly buried somewhere on the grounds.

Academy director Barbara Grant says her research indicates no students were killed there and there were no mysterious fires. She says the dark sap-stained trees have only added hype to a myth the academy has desperately tried to dispel. Tales of bleeding trees, ghostly figures, and cries in the night have forced the academy to keep its gates closed and locked after hours because of all of the curious teenagers.

Wheelock Mission is said to be haunted.

Declared a National Historic Landmark in 1966, Wheelock Mission and Academy has been on Oklahoma's most endangered historic properties since 1993 and in 2000 it became one of America's eleven most endangered historic places. The Choctaw Nation over the years has restored one of the smaller remaining structures, LeFlore Hall, into a small museum.

All that haunts Wheelock Mission are the years of neglect and abandonment that allowed it to fall victim to the power of imagination.

For a tour of the grounds or museum hours call (580) 746-2139.

Size Does Matter
Poteau

What difference does a foot make when you're looking up at a rise in the terrain that's 1,999-feet tall? Well, for the town of Poteau, it's the difference between a hill and a mountain. Add those 12 inches and Poteau loses its claim of having the world's tallest hill. All there would be is another small mountain, which is a common sight in the rolling landscape of southeastern Oklahoma. Having Cavanal Hill not only raises eyebrows but also heightens the town's ability to be seen and heard.

In recent years, the peak of Cavanal Hill has become the site of antennas and numerous cell towers, providing some of the best television reception and the clearest cell phone signals for a 20- to 30-mile radius. During earlier decades, the park on top of the hill had a shelter house where many people went to watch TV.

The top of the hill is a flat plateau that is twenty degrees cooler and has a lookout for beautiful views of Lake Wister and the mountains of Sugar Loaf, Poteau, and Ouachita National Forest. Cavanal is also the site of Poteau Public School's grueling Five Miler foot race in November.

The hill's name, Cavanal, is French meaning "cave," and refers to the coal mines that reside on its eastern side. The rise in the earth caught the attention of Thomas Nuttal of Boston in 1819 while he was studying plant life in the area. He spent a lot of time talking to the local Indians and French trappers about the marvels hidden on or within the hill. The trappers pointed out the small lakes and wildlife near the peak, while the Indians told stories of the roars that could be heard coming from deep within the caves lower on the hill.

Poteau officials first realized it might have the tallest hill prior to World War II when high school students from Leflore County participated in an exchange project with students from England, who bestowed the title on the hill. It wasn't until 1952 that the Poteau Chamber of Commerce decided to research the British students' claim of Cavanal being the world's largest hill and learned from the British Geological Society that a hill was less than 2,000 feet above the local terrain; anything above that was considered a mountain. Geography books and other printed material also indicate Cavanal holds the title, according to the chamber. For more information call (918) 647-9178.

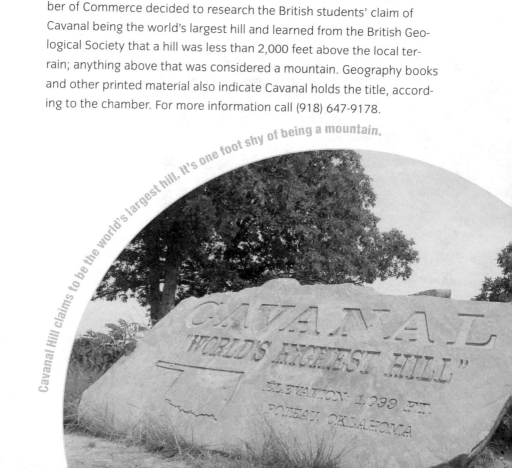

Cavanal Hill claims to be the world's largest hill. It's one foot shy of being a mountain.

Dog Is Man's Best Friend?

Spiro

James Fetters has spent more than a decade facing one of his biggest fears everyday with his job at the City of Spiro. When he'd get dispatched to make a pick up, panic would race through his veins and that traumatic childhood memory would surface to dog him. Would this be the day he'd lose his face-off with man's best friend? Armed with gloves and a noose pole, Fetters would reluctantly ease into the driver's seat of his Animal Control truck and head off on the call. It's tough being the city's dogcatcher when you are afraid of the canine species.

Dogcatcher James Fetters gets ready to brave a day at work.

"I don't dislike dogs, I'm just afraid of 'em. Especially, them little ones that bark all time and act like they're going to bite ya," said the sixty-year-old native of this town of about twenty-two hundred people.

For twelve years, Fetters was the full-time dogcatcher and meter reader. Now, he's a full-time meter reader and helps out occasionally with catching stray dogs.

Fetters's fear of dogs is no secret around town. If someone inquires about the dogcatcher, someone else will say, "Did you know he's afraid of dogs?"

Although the townsfolk all speak fondly of Fetters, they are quick to tell about how he has been seen chasing down stray dogs while driving his truck with his right hand and holding the noose pole out the driver's window with his left hand.

"Why risk it, when you don't have to?" he said smiling.

Fetters said he doesn't like guns, so he doesn't want to use the tranquilizer gun.

"Even if I did, I'd have to chase down the dog and a lot of times that darn tranquilizer doesn't work. You think they're down, but they ain't," he said.

Fetters said when he first started, he was sent out on forty calls a week but now it's about down to twenty, and most of the dogs end up on Boothill, the pet cemetery. Jimmy Smith, now the full-time dogcatcher, said any time Fetters got into trouble, "he'd call me and I'd take care of it."

So with this fear, why did Fetter ever take the job to begin with? He said the city asked him. Fetter has worked for the city most of his life. He also drove the dump truck for years, but now he is looking forward to his dog days of retirement just a few years away.

Earthly Wonders
Spiro

Rumors during the Great Depression that Spanish gold had been buried in mounds outside of Spiro lured six treasure hunters into the area. The men secured a mining lease where several unexplained mounds formed a circle around a plaza in a field northeast of town. The men were unaware of the actual gold mine they were about to uncover. The loot, however, wasn't a chest full of gold doubloons. Instead, they unearthed the remains of an American Indian culture dating from A.D. 850 through 1450.

Soon after the men started mining, they began to find spectacular artifacts, including conch shells and copper that in prehistoric times were the gold and diamonds of their commerce. Although the treasure seekers knew they had found valuable items, they had no idea of the historical and cultural magnitude of their discovery. They had uncovered one of the most significant prehistoric Indian sites east of the Rocky Mountains. Regrettably, the treasure hunters only cared about profiting off their relics and took only the things that they thought were valuable. Other items such as prehistoric lace and other textiles were disregarded and trampled on during their dig.

By the time the treasure hunters' lease expired in 1935, the legislature had banned the sale of the relics, and archaeologists from the University of Oklahoma were allowed to lead a controlled excavation of the site at what became known as the Spiro Mounds. The scientists salvaged, recorded, and preserved what was left. They found items such as copper, shell beads, conch shells, stone tools, baskets, pearls, textiles, and a variety of stone effigy pipes. The copper was traced to the Great Lakes, the shell beads to the Gulf of California, and the conch shells to the Gulf of Mexico. These discoveries indicated that the Spiro Indians had an extensive trade network linking a variety of cultures across the continent.

Had the treasure seekers not been so greedy, they could have found lasting fame well beyond monetary value.

Some of the relics sold by the treasure seekers can be found in private collections now displayed in museums across the country. Much of the artifacts archaeologists excavated from the site are on display there in the Interpretive Center at Spiro Mounds Archaeological Center. The Spiro Mounds and center are located 2.5 miles east of Spiro on Highway 9 and 4 miles north on Spiro Mounds Road. For more information call (918) 962-2062.

Exploring the Spiro Mounds.

IT'S ONLY A TREE FOR GOD'S SAKE

The Bible has been at the core of many disputes over time so nobody should be surprised that it found its way into a 1937 controversy over whether the redbud should be the state's official tree. This time the heated debate erupted between a few of the state's women's clubs when it was learned that Gov. E. W. Marland was going to sign a bill that gave the redbud the official title.

But Marland balked at the signing after he received a telegram from a woman who at the time was president of the National Federation of Women's Clubs opposing the action. She warned that such an act would be inappropriate because it would honor the tree Judas used to hang himself. But the club president of the Tulsa Garden Club began a crusade to plant as many as possible of the controversial trees in Tulsa. She reportedly said that "to glorify the tree that ended the greatest villain of all time seems to me to be quite fitting."

The controversy made the headlines locally and nationally before a horticulturist from Oklahoma A&M College stepped into the fray to give his two cents. He explained that Oklahoma redbud is native to the state and could not be the tree that Judas used. He also cited a sixteenth-century herb book that claimed it was a wild carob tree that Judas used. The horticulturist contended references of Judas using a redbud are merely legend.

The opposition wasn't convinced and offered up the oak or elm tree as better symbols of the state's pioneer spirit, but their suggestion was ignored. Instead, the Legislature in its resolution to adopt the tree stated that it was in fact the redbud and its beautiful foliage that greeted the pioneers as they journeyed across the rolling hills and plains. The redbud was a tree that when it bloomed each spring became the emblem of the eternal renewal of life and gave hope to the tired heart of the settlers in a new land, it stated. It didn't hurt that the governor's wife supported the redbud. A week after the controversy arose, the tree was declared the official state tree.

Although the Bible was the impetus for the debate, nowhere in it does it mention the kind of tree, if any, Judas used to hang himself. It only states that he betrayed Jesus for thirty pieces of silver and later threw the money into the temple and left to go hang himself.

The House That Uncle Sam Built

Swink

The district Choctaw chief's house is not just another old log home nestled in a rural Oklahoma town. It's the oldest home in the state that still rests on its original site. It has been in the hands of the Swink family on and off since the 1890s, long after its original owner, Choctaw chief colonel Thomas LeFlore locked the doors, took the keys, and left town.

The house was one of three built for district chiefs as a result of the 1830 Treaty of Dancing Rabbit Creek when the Choctaws were forced to relocate to Oklahoma from Mississippi, says Lila Swink, who lives in a modern log house about fifty yards away on the eighty-acre site. Officials believe the house was completed in 1837. It is the only house still in existence from that era, according to Swink. During the sixteen years

Lila Swink stands on the porch of her husband's ancestor's home.

Chief LeFlore lived there, he farmed the area plantation style with slaves. The homestead was called the Thousand Acre Farm. The house, which has had some restoration, is operated by the Swink Historical Preservation Association, of which Lila is a founding member.

It was Lila's late husband's grandfather, David Randall Swink, who brought his Choctaw wife to live in the house where she gave birth to their eight children. Swink founded the town in 1902 when the railroad came through. Swink's son, Henry lived in it until 1917, when he was killed and the house was passed on to other families. Between the occupation of Chief LeFlore and the Swinks, the homestead was a focal point of Confederate activities during the Civil War. There also was a pioneer missionary who performed marriages at the house.

If the walls of this historic house could talk, surely they'd tell a tale rich with the elements of a good epic novel—wealth, war, birth, death, marriage, deterioration, and pillage.

In 1960 the Oklahoma Historical Society gained control of the house and its possessions. State budget cuts in 1994, however, resulted in the closure of the house, and the historical society removed the possessions. The same year, the Swink Historical Preservation Association assumed ownership and hopes one day to have the possessions returned. But until then, the house is empty and can be viewed for free. It is located ½ mile north of the Swink Post Office on U.S. Highway 70, then 1 mile east before turning south on a gravel road to the first paved driveway.

A Pilgrimage to the Holy Land
Talihina

Every year hundreds of thousands of pilgrims travel from around the globe to the Middle East to visit biblical landmarks, from Mount Sinai to Jerusalem. However, people don't need to go abroad to pay homage to those holy places; just pack a lunch and go to the southeast—of Oklahoma, that is.

With nothing else around on Highway 63 just east of Talihina except open pasture and the Kiamichi Mountains looming in the distance, the Open Air Prayer and Bible Museum stands out as Goliath did to David. There are three crucifixion-size crosses and a brick wall with seven arches—a number of biblical perfection, as the hand-painted sign states—separating the museum from the two-lane highway.

A stone footpath engraved with each book of the Bible encircles the crosses. On one side of the pasture is a replica of Jesus's empty tomb with a large boulder lying next to the opening, which has a glass door and a deadbolt lock. Why did the disciples trouble themselves with lugging that monstrous boulder when they had the convenience of a heavy door with a deadbolt? But as has been said before, "God works in mysterious ways."

Walking over to the opposite side, visitors will pass two stone plaques displaying the Lord's Prayer and the Ten Commandments. A small building, glassed in on one side, houses the three-part Bible museum: the Ark of the Covenant, the Old Testament, and the New Testament. Peering through the glass of the Old Testament part, visitors will notice a plethora of figures representing different stories of the Old Testament: Daniel in the lion's den, tiny frogs from the plague, Moses with the Ten Commandments, Noah on his ark. On the New Testament side, along with the numerous figures of Jesus at different stages of life, is a silver-bedecked angel bearing a striking resemblance to a GI Joe figure strumming serenely on a harp.

Although it's not in the Middle East, the Open Air Prayer and Bible Museum, located on an open pasture riddled with small holes that house nonpoisonous snakes and other small animals, still offers an unusual pilgrimage—a journey to the Holey Land of southeastern Oklahoma.

Hopefully the angel was also a lock pick.

CHRIST'S EMPTY TOMB
AN ANGEL OF THE LORD CAME
AND ROLLED AWAY THE STONE. MATT 28:2

OKIE TALK

"Don't get the idea our language is a revolt against proper American English. This isn't the case 'atall.' Most of we Okies are bilingual, speaking both our vernacular and proper talk where the occasion arises," writes author Stoney Hardcastle of Wilburton, Oklahoma.

Here is a list of some words commonly heard in conversations throughout the state, courtesy of *Okie Dictionary,* by Stoney Hardcastle.

aim:	I aim to do it.
air:	bow and air.
anuff:	Got anuff?
bidy:	She sunburned her bidy.
bobbed:	a bobbed-war fence.
bumfuzzled:	confused.
bub:	Change the light bub.
cheer:	Pull up a cheer.
come-mere:	Come-mere a minute.
dainz:	She loves to dainz.
drug:	He drug a rope.
extry:	You have an extry dollar?

farred:	Got farred off the job.
fer:	How fer is it?
git:	Git going.
hard:	I hard a good hand.
hep:	Need a little hep?
ignurunte:	He's ignurunte.
jest:	jest because.
morrow:	morrow morning.
okrey:	I luv fried okrey.
pert near:	Pert near done.
rench:	Rench your hair.
shore:	I shore anuff wuz there.
sop:	Sop my bisquits in gravy.
tar:	Had a flat tar.
u'all:	U'all come here.
vittles:	Them good tasting vittles.
whupping:	He got a good whupping.
yonder:	yonder there.
yurp:	France is in yurp.

FRONTIER COUNTRY

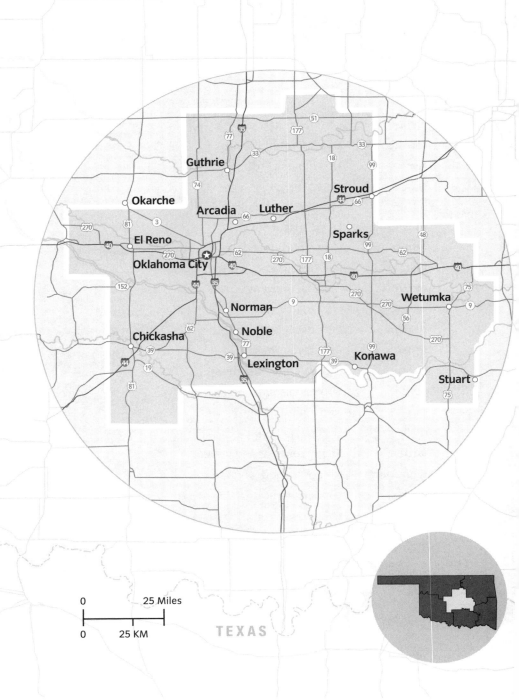

Guthrie
Okarche
Arcadia
Luther
Stroud
El Reno
Sparks
Oklahoma City
Wetumka
Norman
Noble
Chickasha
Lexington
Konawa
Stuart

0   25 Miles
0   25 KM

TEXAS

FRONTIER COUNTRY

Whoever said, "All roads lead to Rome" obviously was not acquainted with the history of Oklahoma's Frontier Country. High noon on April 22, 1889, found fifty thousand settlers lined up on the Kansas border, awaiting the rifle shot or cannon boom that signaled the designated time for legal entry into the unassigned lands that would eventually become Oklahoma. A frenzied chaos ensued with every person on foot, horseback, or train, vying for prime land and battling the "Sooners," the people who unlawfully hid out all night on the unassigned lands in order to get the best land.

Fortunately, visitors to Oklahoma today don't have to wait along the border for a gun blast to signal that they may enter. Visitors to Frontier Country can come across the border any time they wish, but like it was for the hordes of settlers in 1889, the heart of Oklahoma is still the "promised land," promising outlandish characters, unusual events, and interesting places.

The heart of Frontier Country and the state capital, Oklahoma City, contains bragging rights in several areas. The only capitol building in the world with an oil well under it is in Oklahoma City, giving new meaning to the term *greasy politician.* That oil might do well to grease the wheels of those pesky, uncooperative, yet oh-so-useful shopping carts, a product of Oklahoma City. Liquid gold is great, but it won't be helpful in another invention spawned and installed in 1935 in Oklahoma City: the parking meter.

If those inventions don't light your fire, maybe the Lighter Museum in Guthrie might do it. Or, you might want to fire up your engines for the Lawnmower Races in El Reno.

Frontier Country offers a wealth of sites to fascinate and entertain anyone. Continue reading and you'll see why Oklahoma was considered the "promised land" to thousands and what it promises today.

Don't Be Square

Arcadia

Did you hear about what happened to the guy who went up to the hayloft in an old round barn? He died trying to find the corners.

That's the joke that volunteer Butch Breger delivers to each visitor who stops at Oklahoma's only round barn located in the tiny town of Arcadia along Route 66. Breger, who is retired, grew up in Arcadia next door to the barn, which has become the most photographed building in the state.

The barn was built in 1898 out of Oklahoma Burr Oak. It is 60 feet in diameter and 43 feet from foundation to the peak of the dome. It has a loft with a wooden floor that is the entire diameter of the barn.

The building is the creation of W. H. Odor. Although to farmworkers his idea reeked of danger, Odor wouldn't let the smell of skeptics ruin his plans. Once the barn was constructed, Odor had trouble getting farmworkers to go into it for any length of time for fear the roof would collapse.

Odor, who came to the state as a settler during the 1889 land run, constructed the barn with oak grown and cut on a nearby farm. The boards were soaked in a nearby creek to make them pliable so they could be wrapped around the frame. Over time, the barn started to deteriorate, and in 1988 efforts to restore the barn began. By 1992 it had reopened looking much like it did when it was originally built ninety years earlier.

There was a time in the 1930s and 1940s that the hayloft was used for dances because of its smooth wooden floor. Breger said there was only one kind of dance that didn't take place upstairs in the round barn—a square dance. Breger smiled. He has plenty more wit waiting to be heard. The barn is located on Route 66 in the middle of town. You can't miss it. Just stop by and take a picture, or if it's not open, go next door and ask for Butch. He'll be glad to open it up. You can also call (405) 396-0824 or visit www.arcadiaroundbarn.org.

The state's only round barn, located on Route 66.

Signs of the Times
Chickasha

Signs of yesteryear blanket a former 1900s dairy farm where Curtis Hart works and lives. They're not signs depicting life as a farmer, but advertisement signs—hundreds of classic metal, porcelain, light bulb, and neon signs that dotted the countryside over the past eighty years. Now they cover the exterior and interior of Hart's old dairy barns and are strategically displayed on posts throughout his seventy-acre pasture. The vast majority of the signs are from the petroleum industry, and the rest are mostly from hotels and restaurants. Hart's place is an outdoor museum of Americana.

Hart calls his place Muscle Car Ranch, which is also home to several muscle cars and the annual "Woodstock" of swap meets. Hart, who is preparing his refurbished 1959 Mack diesel truck for a road trip, said that he didn't set out to create Muscle Car Ranch; it created itself out of his desire to own his own mechanic's shop, where he could blare rock 'n' roll music as he pumped life back into vehicles, old and new. The signs, which can be seen by the motorists traveling on the turnpike, started as a way to bring color to the old farm, he said. But the signs took on a life of their own. Hart said he found himself spending more time gathering, restoring, and erecting them.

Hart owns the only two remaining Body by Fisher Napoleonic Coach porcelain signs. The Smithsonian inquired about one, but Hart said he wasn't willing to donate it. Among his other great finds is a 30-foot porcelain neon Chevrolet Bow-Tie sign from 1942. There were only four made for General Motors, he said. Also among his collection are an enormous Clock Inn Motel, a sign from Route 66 that weighs 4,000 pounds and is 15 feet wide; a landmark Patio Charcoal Hamburger sign; and a 1950s Maverick Motel sign.

The annual, four-day Woodstock swap meet features muscle cars and a concert by hall-of-fame rock 'n' roll bands. In past years the

Curtis Hart stands outside one of the buildings on his farm, which has one of only four Chevrolet Bow-Tie signs on its roof.

entertainment included the Turtles, Jefferson Airplane, Grass Roots, Byrds, Paul Revere & the Raiders, Dr. Hook, Bad Company, and many others. The swap meet provides an outlet for not only the sale and trade of muscle cars, but also for automotive parts and nostalgic memorabilia. Tens of thousands of people attend the event, many of whom spend the entire weekend on the ranch. There are 150 acres of free parking and camping facilities with showers. For more information on the next event, visit www.musclecarranch.com.

Mowing Down the Competition

El Reno

When folks in this small town west of Oklahoma City start racing to get on their lawnmowers, it's unlikely that they're anxious to mow their yards. In fact, most are headed to a designated dirt track at the edge of town. At first glance the group and their souped-up riding lawnmowers look like a landscaping business on steroids. But as the drivers of the single-seated vehicles rev their engines and don their helmets and protective body gear, it is clear this sport of dirt-track racing on modified riding lawnmowers is serious business.

The El Reno Grascar Lawnmower Racing Association is as big to some Okies as NASCAR is to race car enthusiasts. Every other Saturday from late April through October you can witness this sport that is mostly full of oversized fellas on pimped-out lawnmowers moving 35 to 45 mph around a dirt track about 270 feet in length. The riding lawnmowers range from nearly stock to extremely modified, and all are missing the cutting blades. They do resemble NASCAR racecars, sort of, with the colorful paint jobs, names, and numbers adorning the exterior. The more advanced vehicles look more like a mini-sprint car than a lawnmower, but there is no mistaking, the engine, maybe a little buffed up, is still that of a lawnmower.

Grascar isn't isolated to just the men. One racer points out there's a teen-aged gal that has a bright pink mower named the *Gangsta Barbie* that she races, and races well, he said. The association has a Powder Puff division in which the women compete, but this gal has won plenty in divisions where she's raced against the boys.

In Oklahoma, it doesn't take much to draw interest or a crowd, and racing lawnmowers is proof of that. In Grascar, Okies take pride in mowing down the competition. For more information about race dates and a map location, go to www.elrenograscar.com.

In this race, the competitors literally mow each other down.

The Elixir Fixer
Guthrie

It's not uncommon to find people in the otherwise clean-cut town of Guthrie asking for cocaine, cannabis, morphine, and opium. People don't hesitate to answer: Just go to the corner of Second and Oklahoma, where the Oklahoma Frontier Drugstore Museum houses the oldest pharmacy in the state, Lillie's Drugstore.

Inside, the walls and shelves are lined with LUG bottles ("Label Under Glass") and other containers, some still containing now-illegal drugs

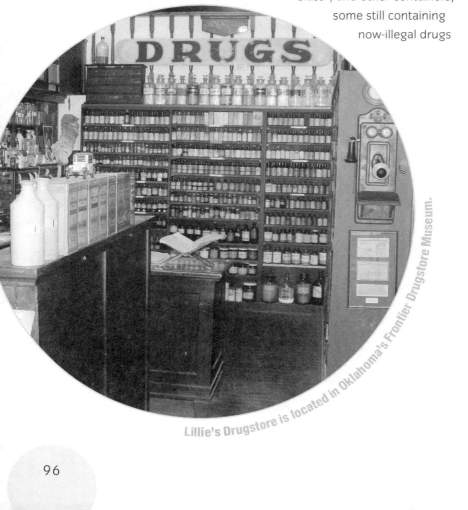

Lillie's Drugstore is located in Oklahoma's Frontier Drugstore Museum.

over one hundred years old as well as a host of alcohol-based concoctions. Many of the former were commonly used during the late 1800s and early 1900s for toothaches, stomachaches, muscle pain, and to enhance the appetite. And some of the home remedies and cure-all tonics have names that sound like a cocktail and they definitely have the alcohol content of one. There is the Peruvian Wine of CoCo and the Tay-Jo Tonic, "medicines" that also could be purchased at one of Little Doc Roberts traveling medicine shows.

Also housed inside the museum is a 1923 authentic, but sadly non-working, soda fountain that is surrounded by an array of 1890s pharmaceutical memorabilia—books, mortars and pestles, old wheelchairs, and bottles of drugs, oils, and tonics.

Some highlighted displays are containers that once held leeches and blood marrow, handmade suppositories, asafetida bags, cacao butter, the Mormon elder's Damiana Wafers, Morely's Hair Restorer, Mary T. Goldman's Gray Hair Color Restorer, and SAGWA, commonly known as snake oil. There are even two framed handwritten prescriptions for alcohol that date back to 1923 and a 1924 hanging on the wall, stating the liquor is to be used only "for medical purposes."

Many of the brands of elixirs found in the drugstore museum are still used today, mostly for flatulence or to cleanse the intestines, such as Fleet Enema and Milk of Magnesium.

Lillie's Drugstore began in a tent pitched by Foress Lillie in the new territory shortly after the gunshot was fired for the land run of 1889. Granted state board license No. 1 in 1908, it served the public from its location at Third and Harrison until it closed and its contents were moved into the historic Gaffney Building at 215 West Oklahoma, as part of the museum which opened in 1992. Pharmacy students from Southwestern Oklahoma State University volunteer at the museum, which is open every day but Monday. Call (405) 282-3024 for hours.

Got a Light?
Guthrie

If you are looking for a place to ponder man's fascination with fire or to view one of the largest collections of flame-making apparatuses, burn some time with Ted Ballard at the National Lighter Museum.

Ballard's collection began with two lighters he got from his grandfather when he was six years old. Now in his seventies, Ballard owns tens of thousands of lighters from around the world, and dating as far back as the mid-1700s. He contends that his collection is more of a symptom of humanity than an unusual hobby, noting that man has always been enthralled by fire and he is no different.

"Man's first reverence was to fire and to those with the knowledge of fire," he says using grand hand gestures and crediting Socrates with the insight.

It takes only a few minutes to realize that Ballard finds a much deeper meaning behind the lighter than most people. He claims that man's first discovery was fire and that man's first invention was a way to make fire—with a lighter.

Ballard boasts about becoming a national expert in the academic world. He said it never fails; each year he gets a call from a college student somewhere in the country wanting a definitive answer to the fiery debate over which came first, matches or lighters. Instead of snuffing out the argument, he said he likes adding a little mental fuel to the fire when talk turns to lighters.

"I tell them that matches are lighters. I then tell them the first lighter is likely the guy that created fire outside of the forces of Mother Nature."

A tour of Ballard's collection is a historical and cultural journey through the evolution of the handheld, flame-making contraptions.

"Lighters depict the social and technical environment of mankind," Ballard said. "From the 1940s through the 1960s lighters were smoking condiments. They even became part of interior decor."

Ballard has probably every style of lighter ever made from an array of perpetual gas lighters first made in the 1700s for public use and found in tobacco shops, men's clubs, and bars to the colorful plastic Bic lighters with the popular "Flick My BIC" slogan that gained popularity in the 1970s.

Ted Ballard shows off some of his unusual lighters in his National Lighter Museum.

Ballard has lighters made by Ronson, Zippo, Dunhill, and even Cartier, which was tagged as the Rolls-Royce of lighters. He even has lighters that were made in occupied Japan and lighters that were used in the Civil War. There are tinder-pistol lighters, watch lighters, pen lighters, themed lighters, music-playing lighters, and Japan novelty lighters. The collection is vast and visually stimulating, drawing you from one theme and era to the next.

There is not a lighter or small fire-making device that Ballard owns that doesn't launch him into a philosophical discussion connecting religion, technology, science, and even politics to the possession of fire. To see his collection and set your mind on fire, call Ballard at (405) 282-3025.

Late Night Power Grab
Guthrie

When two million acres of Indian Territory were open for grabs on April 22, 1889, it took about six hours to turn a section of the vast prairie into one of the nation's largest cities west of the Mississippi. The town of Guthrie, named after Judge John Guthrie, instantly sprouted from nothing to a population of ten thousand as settlers scrambled to stake their land claims. Within a couple of years, Guthrie had become the "Queen of the Prairie," a prominent city with nearly all the amenities of cities back east. She was the territory's capital and when Oklahoma became a state in 1907, she became the state capital. But the grabbing wasn't over.

As the state capital, Guthrie became home to brutal state politics— Republicans versus Democrats. Guthrie was a strong Republican city, while the population of the rest of the state was mostly Democrat. For years, the territory's Democrat governors were not happy about residing in such a Republican city. The state's first governor, Democrat

Charles Haskell, had all he could take of what he called the propaganda being spewed by Guthrie's pro-Republican newspaper, the *Oklahoma Capital,* the foremost newspaper in the state. Haskell threatened to move the state's capital unless the publisher stopped the political attacks. The threat was ignored, the newspaper continued taking jabs at the Democrats, and a few years later a statewide election was called and a bill to relocate the capital was on the ballot.

The State Capital Publishing Company Museum is the former site of the Oklahoma Capital newspaper.

Guthrie tried to lure legislators to stay by building a grandiose Legislative Hall. It wasn't enough, however, to break the statewide Democrat voting bloc, and on June 11, 1910, voters overwhelmingly decided to move the capital to Oklahoma City. It's been said that Governor Haskell wanted so badly to leave what he called the "Republican nest," that in the middle of the night, and before all the votes were all counted, he grabbed the state seal and record book of executive acts and took them to Oklahoma City.

Despite the efforts of the *Oklahoma Capital's* publisher, the demise of the newspaper followed that same year.

The hall built to affect the vote, now a Scottish Rite Masonic Temple, is located at 900 East Oklahoma and is open for tours Monday through Friday. Call (405) 282-1281 for more information. The State Capital Publishing Company building, home to the *Oklahoma Capital,* is now a publishing museum. It is located at 301 West Harrison. For more information call (405) 282-4123. Both buildings are among Guthrie's numerous structures listed on the National Register of Historic Places.

The largest Scottish Rite Masonic Temple in the country.

SOONER OR LATER SOME THINGS CHANGE

The origin of Oklahoma's nickname puzzles me. It does have historic significance but not necessarily one to brag about. That didn't stop the state. After the University of Oklahoma (OU) named its popular football team the Sooners, Oklahoma's official nickname became the Sooner State. Outsiders still scratch their heads when they hear Okies proudly refer to themselves as Sooners, or better yet belt out the university's fight song, "Boomer Sooner."

"I'm a Sooner born and Sooner bred, and when I die, I'll be Sooner dead," is the main line of the song.

A Sooner, you ask? You mean you don't know what a Sooner is? Don't worry, many people in the state don't know what a Sooner is either. In the late 1800s admitting you were a Sooner wasn't a good thing and it could cost you a run-in with the law and a loss of property.

You see, sooners, also known as moonshiners, were people who used the light of the moon to sneak onto unassigned land during the late land rushes and hide in the trees and bushes so they would be in position to claim prime land. By law, settlers wanting land had to participate in a land run by lining up and waiting for a blast of a shotgun before they could claim a piece of land. Many times a settler would legally rush to a site and spend time staking a claim only to find out it was already taken. Settlers didn't like sooners. If caught, a sooner had to face the law and relinquish the land. Sooners had the reputation of being despicable people.

Only time and a successful athletic program can take a name with such negative origins and resurrect it into a label synonymous with winning. Today, it is a name proudly worn by Okies.

A Tale from the Crypt

Konawa

The tale of Katherine Cross has reigned over the small town of Konawa since 1917. Not everyone remembers her exact name or what type of person she was, but everyone remembers and takes liberty with the meaning behind her epitaph and how this legendary teenager met her demise.

Nobody remembers who Katherine Cross was, but her death has become folklore.

FRONTIER COUNTRY

Cross was born in 1899 and died a suspicious death about six months after her eighteenth birthday. Sadly, not many townsfolk attended her burial or even spoke about her afterward. She likely would have been forgotten long ago if it wasn't for her parents. They knew the only way to keep her memory alive was to remind everyone about how she died. So, they inscribed on her tombstone, "Murdered by human wolves." In the decades since her death, the epitaph became the impetus for an array of death stories befitting a campfire setting. The tales ranged from her body being found ripped into pieces by werewolves to her being the victim of a gang of drunken Ku Klux Klan members.

A 1917 article in the *Seminole County News* reveals that Konawa doctor A. H. Yates was arrested for performing a "criminal operation," presumably an abortion, on Cross that resulted in her death. The article also mentions that Yates and Fred O'Neal, a local schoolteacher, had been charged two months earlier for the death of another eighteen-year-old girl, whose death was also suspicious and led to exhumation of her body for an autopsy. It was concluded that this girl's death also occurred due to complications from a "criminal operation" conducted by Yates.

The human wolves were not supernatural creatures hunting under the moonlight or ruffians on an alcohol-induced rampage. Instead, they were respected members of the community. Shame probably helped fuel the folklore that continues today.

The legendary gravestone can be found in the Konawa and Violet Cemetery northwest of Konawa. Take Highway 39 and go north on Section Road N3500. The cemetery is on the east side just north of Section Road E1410.

A Bug's Life
Lexington

A giant black spider stands poised in a pasture along U.S. Highway 77, one-half mile north of Lexington. US 77 is one of the major routes out of Lexington, so arachnophobes may want to select a different route to avoid getting tangled in a web of fear.

The 15-foot-high spider is the creation of Leroy Wilson, who created it out of an old VW bug car. Its six spindly legs are made of iron tubing. He placed it in a pasture next to the highway to guard over his enormous Volkswagen salvage business, which once boasted of having the world's largest stock of VW parts. From 1978 until Wilson's death in 2000, the business housed a graveyard of twenty-five hundred VWs ranging from bugs to Jettas. Now the only things left are an empty salvage yard covered with for sale signs and the unusual spider that from afar has a formidable presence.

The business may be gone but the guardian VW has been salvaged.

TEST HOW OKIE YOU ARE

What year did Oklahoma achieve statehood?
1907—1889—1901

(answer: 1907)

How many states border Oklahoma?
6—4—3

(answer: 6; Texas, New Mexico, Colorado, Kansas, Missouri, and Arkansas)

What is the state beverage?
Sarsaparilla—Root beer—Milk

(answer: Milk)

Twenty-four percent of Oklahoma's land is covered in forest.
True or False?

(answer: True)

How does Oklahoma rank in the nation for total number of American Indian residents?
First—Second—Third

(answer: Second)

What is the capital of Oklahoma?
Guthrie—Tulsa—Oklahoma City

(answer: Oklahoma City)

What is the license plate motto?
Oklahoma is OK—America's Heartland—Wind, Water, and Air

(answer: Oklahoma is OK)

Oklahoma has the most man-made lakes in the country.
True or False?

(answer: True)

The state capitol sits on top of an oil well.
True or False?

(answer: True)

What is the state insect?
Mosquito—Locust—Bumblebee

(answer: Bumblebee)

Imitation Is the Sincerest Form of Flattery
Luther

Around the bend on rural Route 66 between Luther and Arcadia sits John Hargrove's homestead. There is no specific signage identifying it, but you'll know it when you come across it. Most people can't help but stop, for their curiosity gets the better of them—is it a site, or just a sight? It's not listed anywhere as anything, but its appearance tells you it's definitely something.

The direction you're headed affects what catches your eye first—is it the unusual lawn ornaments representing Route 66 icons? Or the old-fashioned gasoline station connected to a larger building that has the front end of a Volkswagen bug protruding from the second story as if it crashed through the exterior? On the corner of the driveway a signpost notes the mileage east to Chicago and Tulsa and west to Winslow, Arizona, and Hollywood. The site is definitely a lure, hooking motorists daily.

A small area on the acreage dubbed by Hargrove as "Volkswagen Acreage" for the half-buried bright red Volkswagen bug is his take on Texas's "Cadillac Ranch." Nearby are reproductions of the two giant arrows once seen on the route in Twin Arrows, Arizona, before they became casualties of the construction of Interstate 40, which mostly parallels the route except in some areas where it literally took portions of Route 66.

Although his homestead is not an official Route 66 site, Hargrove, a sixty-two-year-old ultramarathoner, welcomes anyone willing to stop and take a peek. To most everyone's surprise, what's on display outside is only a small taste of what he has stored inside the seven-thousand-square-foot, two-story metal building that is sectioned into his office, workshop, and a partial museum. The latter resembles a 1950s diner strategically decorated with antiques and more replicas of Route 66 icons.

John Hargrove and replica of Myrtle, a giant kachina doll.

"I'm not trying to be original. I'm just trying to revive what was out there," said Hargrove, who built everything on his property by hand, including another smaller metal building in which he lives.

He's just completed a replica of Myrtle, a giant kachina that once stood outside the Queenan Trading Post in Elk City. The doll now stands outside the National Route 66 Museum there. Hargrove said his next plan is to duplicate one of Route 66's drive-in theaters on the back wall, where he will show movie videos.

Hargrove said he likes how his place gets visitors thinking about the hot spots on the route during its heyday. Not many of the historic high-way's icons exist anymore due to the creation of Interstate 40. But in recent years, nostalgia for the highway has pumped some life back into it with a growing number of tourists both domestic and foreign experiencing the route by bus, motorcycle, and car.

"I'm the only one [who] has preserved some of these icons," he said. "You don't have to drive the entire route to see them. When people stop here they get a bigger picture of Route 66 and what it had and still has."

Hargrove's artwork may be just a reproduction of the real thing, but you have to admit, he sure has found a unique method to fuel a new appreciation for the highway.

"Most people tour Route 66. I live it," he said.

Hargrove doesn't have business hours. He said that if the driveway gate is open, knock on the door, and he'll let you get a kick out of his tribute to Route 66.

Everything is Coming Up Roses

Noble

Buying a bouquet of roses from Nancy and Joe Stine is always a rocky experience. You would think that would hamper their sales. It hasn't. In fact, people flock to their shop in Noble for that very reason—to buy Oklahoma's rose rocks.

Since the Stines opened the Timberlake Rose Rock Museum in Noble two decades ago, visitors have come to the facility located in a converted five-room bungalow to not only to buy rose rocks, but to also view the couple's massive collection of artwork which ranges from jewelry to bouquet sculptures that suspend dime-size rose rocks on steel wires connected to a larger base rock. The artwork resembles something you might find in a Hallmark or curio shop.

Nancy is a retired executive secretary, and Joe holds a master's degree in geology. They seem eager to show off their museum and workroom to unexpected tourists. Their shop is filled with the reddish rocks formed in petal-like clusters that resemble roses.

The place is quaint and more of an educational experience than a museum. While Nancy shows off the artwork, Joe takes visitors through the geological history and Native American legend on how the rock was formed.

The Stines were not the first to find the value in the rocks. The late Fred Shobert, a Noble farmer, was the first person known to be selling the rocks after finding truckloads of them on his land, according to local writer Shelley Brinsfield. He trucked them throughout the state and across the county selling them for $1.50 apiece or 50 cents for a pound, Brinsfield writes. He even decorated a wall of his farmhouse with them. He died in 1972 before Noble was dubbed the rose rock capital by former Gov. George Nigh in 1983.

The Stines sort of took off from where Shobert ended, continuing the sale of the unusual rock formations, which by the way, can be found for free if you are willing to hunt the gullies and ditches of eroded areas or construction sites. They're buried in abundance beneath the earth. The best time to look is during a heavy rain. A single rock can range in size from smaller than a dime to larger than a dinner plate. Some rose rock clusters have measured more than 3 feet in diameter. One of the magical aspects of these unusual formations is the glittering glow they emit when hit by sunlight. They are actually sandy crystals of barium sulphate, and the reddish ones can only be found in central Oklahoma along an 80-mile strip stretching from Pauls Valley to Guthrie. Because it is exclusive to Oklahoma, the rose rock was named the state's official rock in 1968. For more than twenty years, Noble has held the annual Rose Rock Festival each year on the first Saturday in May. The museum is located at 419 South Highway 77. Call (405) 872-9838 or visit www .roserockmuseum.com.

Nancy Stine holds a cluster of Oklahoma rose rocks.

The Legend of the Rose Rock

According to Joe Stine, there are two Cherokee legends surrounding the creation of the red rose rock, which is found only in Oklahoma.

Cherokee Rose

The rose rock is God's way of commemorating the brave Cherokee Indians who died on the Trail of Tears journey to Oklahoma. The trek was a forced migration of about seventeen thousand Cherokees to Indian Territory by the government after gold was discovered in Georgia. About four thousand Cherokees died.

The legend says that God took the drops of blood from the Indian braves and the tears from the Indian maidens that stained the ground of the trail and turned them into stones in the shape of a Cherokee Rose in their honor. Stine said that is why there are so many rose rocks in Oklahoma—it is the end of the Trail of Tears.

Singing Bird and the Roses of Rock

There was a young Indian maiden named Singing Bird, who entertained at the campfire with her beautiful singing voice. But on the night of the Harvest Moon, Singing Bird was overcome by fever, an illness too strong for the medicine man to cure, and "her spirit passed on to the land beyond the sun."

Singing Bird's passing plunged the tribe into mourning for days. Women wailed, and supplications were offered to the Great Spirit, whose wrath these people could not understand, Stine said.

Members of the tribe began building altars out of sandstone and on the tenth day, the Great Spirit spoke, turning the red rocks into a bouquet of red rock roses as an eternal symbol of the "maiden's ever present spirit, love and compassion for the Great Spirit."

Source: *The Rose Rock of Oklahoma*, written by Nancy and Joseph Stine

What an Ego!
Norman

The University of Oklahoma (OU) has been accused of having quite an ego regarding its nationally acclaimed Sooners football team. And those who say the university's Memorial Stadium is filled with big heads couldn't be more right. For fifty years, what is now determined to be the largest dinosaur skull ever discovered was stored in crates beneath the stadium seats. The skull, which holds the Guinness World Record as the largest head, measures 10.5 feet tall and belongs to a *Pentaceratops*.

"Can you imagine that all this time we've literally been sitting on this?" asked museum volunteer, Ralph Venk.

Venk said the crates ended up under the stadium seats because there was no other spot large enough to store all of them. It wasn't

The Sam Noble Museum of Natural History houses the largest dinosaur skull of any land animal.

Horns and Frills

until they started assembling the bones that anyone realized how big the skull was. The *Pentaceratops*, which means five-horned face, is an herbivorous dinosaur native to North America. This particular skeleton was originally found in New Mexico in 1941 by an OU archaeologist professor, but *Pentaceratops* were living in Oklahoma more than seventy-five million years ago, Venk said.

So, when Oklahoma Sooners talk about having a big head, they're not necessarily talking about team spirit. The heady find is now displayed in the Sam Noble Museum of Natural History at the University of Oklahoma, located on the corner of Chautauqua Avenue and Timberdell Road. For more information call (405) 325-4712 or visit www.snomnh.ou.edu.

Chicken Tender

Okarche

There is something to be said for Eischen's Bar, the oldest operating establishment in the state. It not only survived Prohibition, but also a fierce fire that gutted it in 1993.

The now bar-restaurant, run by fifth generation Eischens, is located at 108 Second Street just off Main Street in Okarche. It's not unusual to find customers lining the sidewalk waiting to gain entry for a cold beer and Eischen's specialty—a whole deep-fried chicken, served in a paper boat on butcher paper.

The establishment has come a long way since it first opened. It's hard to say which bar tale captures the essence of this historic landmark that Ed Eischen's great-grandfather opened as a territorial saloon in 1896. It's likely that a combination of all the stories depict the Eischens' ability to attract customers.

There was the bar's crowd-drawing centerpiece, a massive Spanish ornate, hand-carved mahogany bar-back that Eischen's great-grandfather purchased in Oklahoma City. The antique piece was originally shipped to California during the gold rush days. Eischen said nobody knows who had it or how it ended up in Oklahoma. The antique bar-back was the featured attraction in the bar until a 1993 fire destroyed all but a small piece that is now showcased in the bar.

There's also been a host of characters known to frequent the place, like Sister Anita, a Felician nun, who sold raffle tickets to bar patrons to raise funds to buy medical equipment for Okarche Memorial Hospital. Instead of saving souls, Sister Anita preyed on the generosities and guilt of the inebriated until she successfully satisfied the fund-raising till with enough dough.

Eischen's is the state's oldest operating bar, now known for its fried chicken.

There also was the bar's connection to the King Can club, which opened in the basement of the oldest IGA grocery store in the state. The store was located next door to the bar and was also owned by the Eischens. The King Can was born in 1964 and for seventeen years bands played dance music, drawing weekend crowds. Most of the weekend customers were from out of town.

But what likely sealed the success of Eischen's Bar stems from the Wednesday night shuffleboard tournaments that started in the 1970s. The winners were awarded a whole chicken covered in a secret coating and fried in a cast iron pan. The chicken was from IGA's unsold inventory each week. The chicken became popular, and the bar began serving it every Wednesday night until it became so popular that Eischen's started serving it seven days a week.

"It started out that people came to the bar to drink beer and occasionally eat chicken. Now, it's people who come to eat the chicken and occasionally have a drink," said Eischen's daughter, Annette.

The bar is known to fry between twenty-five hundred and three thousand chickens a week, she said. The IGA has since closed and become part of the expanded bar.

The day the business reopened after the fire, customers were lined up along the sidewalk before lunch and into the evening for dinner, she said.

The fire may have destroyed nearly all of the bar and the historic mementos and photographs, but it only heated up the nostalgia and customer enthusiasm to get to Eischen's before the chicken runs out.

A Matter of Timing
Oklahoma City

Noted journalist Carl C. Magee spent his career meeting deadlines. So nobody was surprised, not even Magee, when he invented a machine that would mark time—for parked vehicles, that is. Shortly after his arrival in Oklahoma City in 1927, Magee took on the task of finding a way to ease the annoyance of the on-street parking congestion in the city's bustling downtown business district. The problem was that downtown workers were parking their vehicles on the streets all day in limited-time parking spaces, leaving customers no place close to the businesses to park.

A 1940s photo of downtown Oklahoma City, where parking meters were first used.

In an attempt to keep track of who parked when, police walked the streets chalking tires with a mark and then returned when the allotted time had expired. If the car hadn't moved, the officer issued a citation. That method, however, generated an abundance of disputes. That's when Magee, then chair of the Oklahoma City Chamber of Commerce Traffic Committee, agreed to take on the challenge of finding a better way to monitor parking.

His solution was the parking meter, a small, windable, coin-activated time machine that would be placed at every parking space. The city leaders pounced on the idea. Pay to park or face the fine—either way it would build their coffers and there would be no more disagreements over the validity of the chalking system.

Not long after Oklahoma City installed the parking meters in their downtown area, cities across the nation began to use them. Today it's hard to find a downtown that doesn't have the single-headed meters, which have changed little from the original design.

The meters haven't totally cured the parking woes in the heavily congested downtowns, or the run-ins with parking meter enforcers—that solution will come in just a matter of time.

FRONTIER COUNTRY

No Chance of Running Out of Gas Here

Oklahoma City

Most state Capitols across the country can't deny that when the Legislature is in session there's a steady production of gas spewing from its chambers. And Oklahoma is no different, except for decades its production of the combustible product was twofold. Besides what was coming from within the building, there was plenty coming from underneath it.

Oklahoma has the only capitol in the world that is surrounded by several working oil wells. The classic Greco–Roman style building was constructed around 1917 and at one time there were twenty-four oil wells on the grounds. Now there are only two left.

The wells were part of the Oklahoma City oil field and, for a period of time in history, held the title of the second most productive field in the country. The Oklahoma Legislature passed a law in 1935 that authorized the capitol grounds to be leased for oil and gas production.

The state's connection to the energy industry is deep. Oil and gas are what made the state and many of its other cities like Tulsa, Ponca City, and Bartlesville. At the south entrance of the capitol stands Petunia No. 1, an enormous oil derrick marking a well that was drilled diagonally so it could tap into an oil pool located a mile and a quarter beneath the government building. Drilled in 1941 in the middle of a petunia flowerbed, Petunia No. 1 spent forty-three years pumping a total of 1.5 million barrels of oil and 1.6 billion cubic feet of natural gas. She was capped in the mid-1980s after going dry. Phillips Petroleum Co. continued to tap the well's natural gas for some time afterward.

Petunia became and remains a symbol of historical significance depicting the important relationship the state had with the oil and gas industry. Some people, however, might argue that there is no need to keep the oil derrick around to reflect that. The politicians do that each time the legislative session reopens.

Let God Do Your Driving

Oklahoma City

It was reported in 1994 that during the first two months of that year, Oklahoma City police stopped several motorists who carried "God's Insurance Policy" on their vehicles. Apparently, the insurance salesman assured customers that the policy he was selling complied with the state law mandating motor insurance. The text of the $285 policy reported it was straight out of the Bible. The policy stated the insurance was issued by "the Father, Son and Holy Ghost." The policy declared it would provide better insurance than other carriers because "fear" was the cause of accidents.

Out of Sync with the Current Times

Oklahoma City

Anyone who enters the living room of Becky Rickard's Oklahoma City home will clearly see that this fifty-four-year-old woman has a fondness for the western days of yesteryear. A tour of the rest of the house, the backyard, and the small storage shed suggests that her fondness may be more of a fixation.

"I should have been born in 1852, instead of 1952. I'm definitely in the wrong era," says this talkative Oklahoma native, whose massive western decor is shy of museum quality, yet much finer than a flea market's medley.

"My family thinks I have a screw loose. Who knows, maybe I do," she said.

Rickard claims it was Barbara Stanwyck in the movie, *Annie Oakley*, that lassoed her love for the Wild West. She proudly points out her Annie Oakley memorabilia, which includes a 1950s board game, photos of Stanwyck, and other Oakley and Western trinkets throughout the house. She even named her Yorkie Phoebe Ann Moses, Oakley's birth name. All of this is merely a smattering of what Rickard has collected over the years. So, it's really unnecessary to question her desire to be called Buckaroo Becky. It kind of makes sense really.

Rickard's (or Buckaroo Becky's) collection includes vintage, restored Rancho Wagon Wheel furniture from the late 1940s and a host of 78-rpm Western albums, which she plays regularly. She has a complete collection of Louis L'Amour books, including his rare book of poetry, along with a 1950s Western-designed chenille bedspread and other furnishings from a room at a now-closed motor lodge in West Yellowstone. She has signed Western art, folk art, classic Western movie posters,

Buckaroo Becky and Phoebe Ann Moses show off their home.

board games, replicas of famous Western sculptures, photos, belt buckles, guns, six hundred Western movie videos, and that's just the beginning. There is not a light-switch cover, clock, bar of soap, or toilet-paper roll holder exempt from the theme. Rickard even grills on a stagecoach-designed charcoaler.

The oddest items are the contents of a wooden box she keeps in the kitchen and her unusual hair dryer. Preserved in that box are the ashes of her late Shetland pony, a paint she named Buffalo Bill's Lighting Bolt. The pony was a gift from a posse of her friends for her fortieth birthday. The pony's saddle, a bridle, and two pairs of chaps (one child-size, the other adult) are displayed in the guest bedroom. The hair dryer? It's a plastic replica of an ivory-handled Colt .45. Its trigger is the on/off switch and it rests in its own holster on the wall near her bathroom sink.

Carting Off the Goods
Oklahoma City

The shopping cart is the most sought-after consumer item at grocery and department stores across the country. Its popularity forces shoppers to race to get their hands on one, especially during busy shopping days or seasons. So it is hard to imagine that such a staple gadget ever had difficulty catching on, but it is true, it did.

In the spring of 1937, Sylvan Goldman, an Oklahoma City grocery store owner, had an idea on how to get shoppers to buy more during each visit. Suspecting that people only bought as much as they could carry around the store, Goldman took the handheld wire basket that customers currently used to cart things around and affixed it to the seat of a wooden folding chair to which he attached wheels. This primitive contraption became his prototype that with relatively little concept change into the carts evolved into what we use today.

Goldman was quite shocked when people shunned his invention, choosing to continue to use and struggle with the cumbersome hand-held baskets. He actually spent as much time trying to convince consumers to try the cart as he did perfecting its practical use. The main hurdle was the consumer's perceived stigma that came with using the cart over the basket. Young women thought it lacked style, men felt weakened by it, and the elderly felt it made them look helpless. To dispel these perceptions, Goldman hired men and women of various ages to push the carts around the store acting as if they were actually shopping. He also hired consumer greeters, who offered up his shopping cart with instructions on how to use it. No, Wal-Mart was not the first store to hire greeters. Goldman even turned to print advertisement to help make his cart appealing. Ads featuring a weary looking woman with a purse in one hand and a heavy wire basket full of goods in the other said: "Basket juggling is a lost art at your Standard Food Stores."

Another use for the innovative shopping cart.

By 1940 consumers embraced the concept and Goldman had a seven-year waiting list for the carts. His first set of carts was called folding basket carriers. The removable handheld wire baskets sat on collapsible metal frames with wheels. By the 1950s, the models evolved into the larger nest cart, which could fit inside one another for storage—the standard carts of today.

One of Goldman's first folding basket carriers is on display at Oklahoma City's Omniplex Science Museum, 2100 NE 52nd Street. Call (405) 602-OMNI for hours.

Dark Deed, Light Loot
Sparks

About all that's left of Sparks, a former railroad town, are the remains of the old rock bank and the story of a 1908 midnight robbery that was more trouble than what it was worth. Named after George Sparks, who operated the Fort Smith & Western Railway, this now rural community sits lonely at the end of a spur on Highway 18—a stark contrast to its bustling times of the early 1900s.

As the legend has it, a gang of robbers decided to break into the bank at midnight while the town was asleep. They concocted a plan that included barbed wire and a small amount of nitroglycerin, items they supposedly stole from the local hardware store. When they arrived at the bank, they rolled out layers of barbed wire in front of the door, creating a prickly shield they figured would slow down lawmen if they arrived before the robbers finished their deed. A cup of nitro was the explosive that would gain the robbers entry into the bank vault. The robbers placed the cup of nitro on top of the vault door next to a candle used to illuminate the way. The idea was simple; detonate the nitro by shooting it. The problem, however, was that the candle wasn't bright enough and none of the robbers could clearly see the cup. They unloaded several rounds of gunfire, missing the target but waking the law. A local lawman rushed to the scene only to be stopped outside by the barbed wire. It didn't, however, stop an exchange of gunfire between the lawman and outlaws. During the hail of gunfire, a bullet hit the nitro blasting away the vault door and most of the paper money. Amid the chaos sparked by the explosion, the robbers grabbed what little they could and escaped into the dark night with a light load of loot.

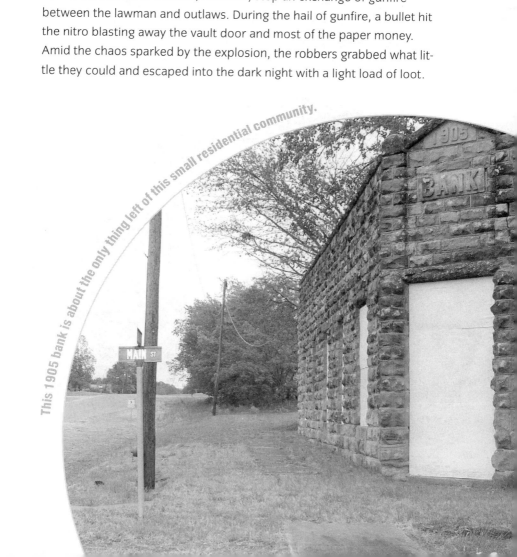

This 1905 bank is about the only thing left of this small residential community.

Cooking Up a Recipe for Success

Stroud

When world traveler Dawn Welch heard about a 1939 landmark eatery on a family visit to Stroud, she had a feeling that the closed Rock Café on Route 66 was something she could really sink her teeth into. It was 1993 and Welch was twenty-four with a hunger to start a business.

Instead of carrying out her initial idea of just buying the restaurant equipment and shipping it to Costa Rica where incentives were offered to entrepreneurs, this former cruise-line employee created a recipe for success by capitalizing on the cafe's rich history and the growing nostalgia for Route 66 landmarks.

Cafe owner Dawn Welch plays checkers with her daughter Alexia and son Paul during a break between lunch and dinner.

FRONTIER COUNTRY

There's nothing fancy about the joint, located at 114 West Main Street, also Route 66. It's comfortable. The locals all know each other. It's a place where checker-board games with pop bottle lids as game pieces sit on the dining counter ready to be used. The booths are small and mementos decorate the walls. Although the menu includes everything from chicken-fried steak to Jagersnitzal and Spaeztle, the locals boast about its greasy hamburger, which has been a Rock Café staple throughout its history.

When the cafe opened in 1939, it was an instant success, becoming the dining spot for travelers. During times of war, it was where GIs had their last meal before they departed and their first upon returning. Couples met their future spouses there, and coast-to-coast truckers made it a regular stop. Before there were CB radios, the cafe was used to relay messages between truckers and their families. It also was a Greyhound bus stop due to its location on the highway. In times of gas and electrical outages, the food was cooked on the indoor fireplace, where cash was often found hidden behind loose bricks. Like many southern establishments during and before the civil rights era, the cafe segregated its customers, serving blacks from a back window.

Through the good, the bad, and the ugly, Welch's ownership and the renewed popularity of Route 66 are creating another chapter of memories for the landmark, drawing a whole new group of customers—foreigners driving the historic highway. Welch recalls the time a Japanese group stopped for a bite and broke out in an Elvis song with the lyrics being the only English they knew. The writers of the Pixar movie, *Cars,* heard of the Rock Café and tapped Welch's personality as the inspiration for the cartoon character, Sally the Porsche, voiced by actress Bonnie Hunt.

Welch's decision to stay in Oklahoma was the one ingredient the Rock Café needed. Now, the world travels to her.

For more information and hours, call (405) 968-3990 or visit www.rockcaferoute66.com.

Bring Out the Big Guns

Stuart

This little town of less than three hundred people didn't need political clout to bring in a big gun to add to their war memorial in 1992. In fact, former mayor Cassel Lawrence said he purposely bypassed the state politicians and went straight to Washington, D.C., with their request that Stuart be sent one of the biggest guns available—a Howitzer M110 self-propelled army tank, that is. Residents knew it would be the perfect thing to top off this rural town's war memorial, setting it apart from all the rest. Well, the big guys in Washington agreed and Stuart was allowed to purchase a tank, one of many taken out of commission and available.

Stuart's war memorial includes a Howitzer M110 self-propelled army tank.

FRONTIER COUNTRY

Before the arrival of the tank, strangers used to drive through Stuart and not realize that they had just driven through the town. Now they are caught off guard by the conspicuous tank strategically positioned across the street from the only visible businesses in the main area of town on Highway 31A, a feed store and a tag agency. The tank sits in a park area next to a small granite war memorial consisting of six granite slabs that form a circle and create a solemn place to view the names of veterans etched on the granite. All of these veterans attended Stuart Public School and the original school bell is mounted above the memorial.

"Erecting this was a big day for a little place like Stuart. This is as good as it gets around here," Lawrence said.

It isn't surprising that the mayor of a town that started off with the Choctaw name, Hoyoyuby, meaning "woman killer," and whose first person buried in the town cemetery was a horse thief had a little prank up his sleeve when he helped army officials determine the alignment of the tank—it's aimed precisely at Stuart's rival town, Calvin.

Tag It
Wetumka

Despite inquiries by strangers, locals don't seem to want to talk much about the unusual house sitting on Highway 9 just inside the city limits of Wetumka.

"It's not that big of a deal," said resident Anita Pasley. "Now our new water tower, that's something."

While indeed it is a nice water tower, it's still kind of hard to overlook the strange looking house sitting there with high visibility and no explanation.

From afar, the small house looks tagged but not with the typical graffiti found in urban areas. As you get closer, you see that it is covered, nearly every bit of it, with old license plate tags. As it happens, it is the former site of the Wetumka Tag Agency. Okay, that makes some sense in a charming way, but why does everyone shy away from talking about it?

The agency apparently moved downtown in the summer of 2005 to a more convenient space inside the Stringfellow True Value Hardware store. Pasley, who became the new operator of the agency after it changed locations, really downplays the house, saying it shouldn't have all those tags on it. She explains that the former agency operator was taking the old tags that were turned in and nailing them to the house. Pasley said she thinks the tags should have been destroyed, but she isn't going to make a fuss.

Town councilman Brent McGee said he thinks the house is kind of cool but doesn't know all of the facts behind why the tags are on the house or why the agency moved. All he knows is the move into the hardware store assures there is always someone available to conduct business for the agency.

The door on the house has only one plate affixed and it reads, TAG N. (Is there a guess as to what that stands for?) With nobody willing to talk about the house, a more appropriate plate would read, DNT ASK.

The former tag agency gets lots of inquiries by strangers driving through town.

There's One Born Every Day, But an Entire Town?

Wetumka

When F. Bam Morrison cruised through Wetumka in the mid-1950s, he left behind something the townsfolk have been laughing at ever since—themselves.

To this day, this fraudster is the reason why the town celebrates Sucker Day. Yes, on the second weekend in September every even year, the town commemorates the day it was hoodwinked by the smooth-talking Morrison, who claimed to be an advance man for a Big Top circus.

Morrison's pitch was that a spectacular circus would be traveling by train through Wetumka in late July. He excited town leaders and merchants as he described a carnival that would not only consume Wetumka, but draw many outsiders.

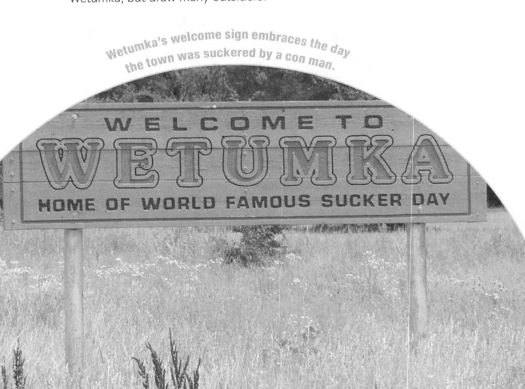

Wetumka's welcome sign embraces the day the town was suckered by a con man.

He convinced merchants to buy advance tickets and advertisements. He explained that those merchants who purchased the advertisements would be repaid two-, even three-fold by the circus that would need to buy large quantities of supplies. Morrison sealed the deal, cash was exchanged, and the town prepared for the circus's arrival.

Bertie Lou Stringfellow said her father, Argie Taylor, was one of the town leaders who planned to make lots of money selling hay to the circus.

"I remember the weather was great that day and the town was full. Carnival food was being prepared while everyone waited anxiously for the circus," she said. "The train finally came but it didn't bring a circus. And when nobody could find F. Bam Morrison, we knew we had been had."

Before the mood could turn too sour, Taylor talked everyone into taking advantage of the circus preparations and celebrating anyway. Newspaper coverage of how the town turned a sting into a wingding spread across the nation—and the official Sucker Day was born. It was such a big deal that even a children's book, *The Flimflam Man,* is based on the event.

According to town councilman Brent McGee, the town wanted Morrison to be parade marshal on the tenth anniversary of Sucker Day. The town searched for Morrison and found him in an Iowa jail. Morrison told town leaders he'd be more than glad to serve as parade marshal if the town would bail him out of jail. And as much as the town leaders thought Morrison would liven up the festival, none were willing to take the risk of getting suckered twice. The word is that they declined Morrison's counteroffer declaring, "We weren't born yesterday."

OKLAHOMA IDOLS

Every state has its rich and famous and Oklahoma is no different. After all, newcomer country-western signer Carrie Underwood, who rose to fame in 2005, isn't the state's only American idol.

Probably the state's most known celebrity is Will Rogers, whose witty way with words won the heart of the nation. He poked fun of his home state with jokes such as: "When the Okies left Oklahoma and moved to California, it raised the I.Q. of both states." And he joked about current events and prominent people. The political arena, however, provided him a platform from which he launched most of his jibes.

"The thing about my jokes is they don't hurt anybody. You can take 'em or leave 'em . . . But with Congress, every time they make a joke, it's a law. And every time they make a law, it's a joke!"

Other Oklahoma idols include the abundance of country music musicians from Reba McEntire and Patti Page to Gene Autry, Garth Brooks, Roger Miller, Toby Keith, and Vince Gill. Other music stars are opera soprano Leona Mitchell, rocker Leon Russell, folk singer Woody Guthrie, and pop bands Hanson and the GAP Band.

Some of the Okies who made it to Hollywood and Broadway are Iron Eyes Cody, James Garner, Tony Randall, Sam Harris, Alfre Woodard, William "Hopalong Cassidy" Boyd, Brad Pitt, Dan Rowen, Ron Howard, Mary Kay Place, Joan Crawford, Rue McClanahan, Megan Mullally, Blake Edwards, Kristin Chenoweth, Amber Valletta, and Bill Hader.

The state has also had more than its share of athletes such as Olympic gold medalists Jim Thorpe for track and Shannon Miller and Bart Conner for gymnastics, LPGA champion Nancy Lopez and PGA champion Bob Tway, Dallas Cowboys quarterback Troy Aikman, NBA star and now jazz guitarist Wayman Tisdale, Cincinnati Reds catcher Johnny Bench, Yankees outfielder Mickey Mantle, and Boston-Milwaukee Braves left-handed pitcher Warren Spahn.

Other notable Okies include former U.S. House Speaker Carl Albert; Alice Mary Robertson, the first Oklahoma woman elected to Congress; journalist Paul Harvey; authors S. E. Hinton, Louis L'Amour and Ralph Ellison; former ambassador Jeane Kirkpatrick; astronauts Shannon Lucid and William Pogue; and the first female Cherokee chief Wilma Mankiller.

Oklahoma also has six Miss Americas—1926 Norma Smallwood, a Cherokee and first American Indian to capture the crown; 1967 Jane Jayroe; 1981 Susan Powell; 1996 Shawntel Smith; 2006 Jennifer Berry; and 2007 Lauren Nelson—and five internationally renowned Native American ballerinas—Yvonne Chouteau, Marjorie Tallchief, Maria Tallchief, Rosella Hightower, and Moscelyne Larkin.

Some of Oklahoma's tarnished idols include its long string of outlaws: Bluford Blue Duck, Jesse James, Belle Starr, and Pretty Boy Floyd to name just a few.

LAKE COUNTRY

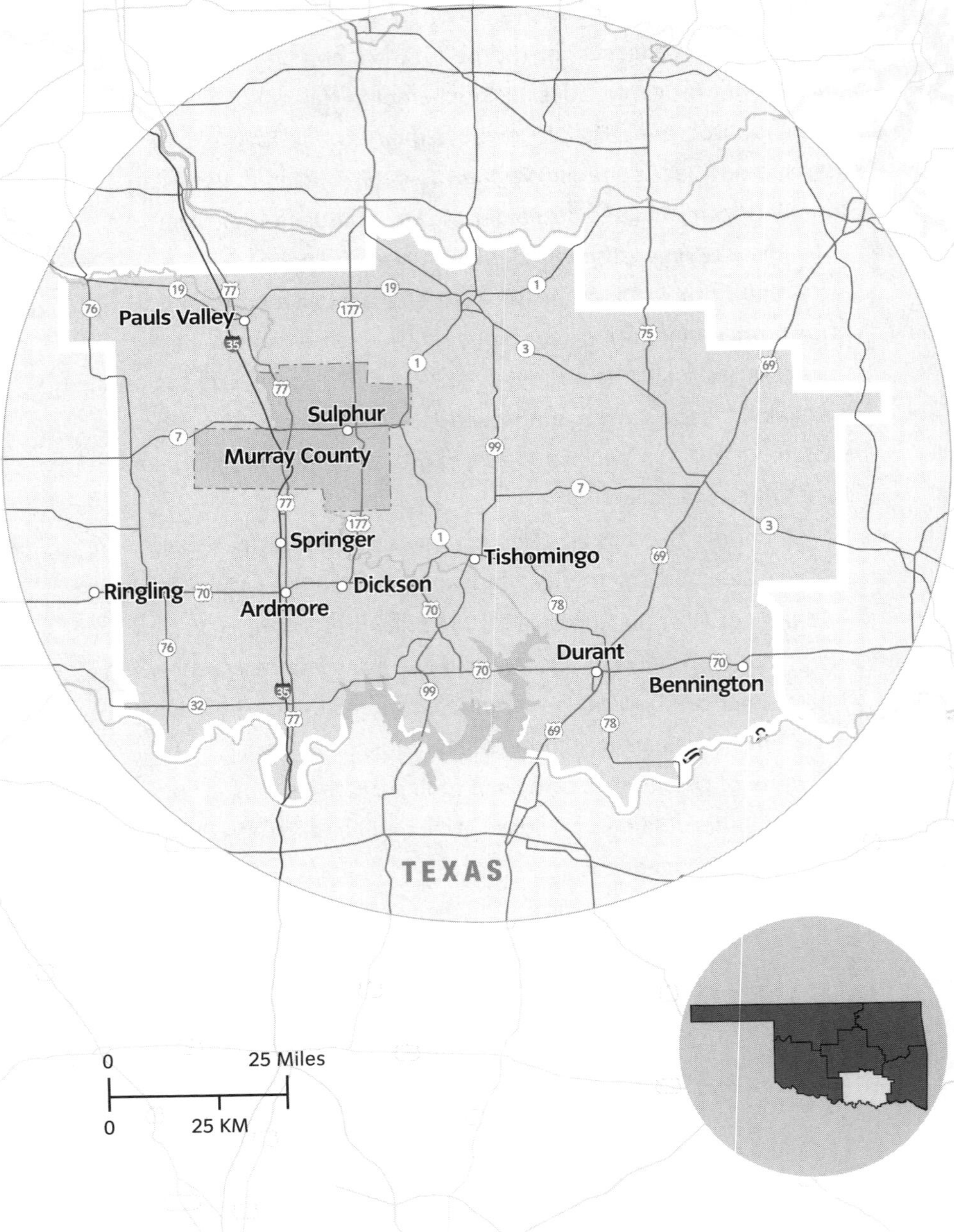

Pauls Valley

Sulphur

Murray County

Springer

Ringling

Dickson

Ardmore

Tishomingo

Durant

Bennington

TEXAS

0 — 25 Miles

0 — 25 KM

LAKE COUNTRY

South central Oklahoma is swimming in nature's creations from the Arbuckle Mountains to the gentle Washita, pristine Blue, and vigorous Red Rivers, which create four recreational lakes not to mention the mineral springs used by the settlers for medicinal purposes. If you're feeling a little under the weather, Sulphur has just the remedy at one of their bathhouses, where you can relax in mineral water. Or, you can visit Vendome Well, where sulphur water is available for consumption to soothe what ails you.

This area of the state is a vacation haven, where the troubles of stress, gridlock, and road rage are nowhere to be found. It's a mecca for fishermen, where they can use a conventional rod and reel at one of the lakes or their bare hands to snag a catfish in one of the noodling contests held in Tishomingo or Pauls Valley. There is even a mysterious side of Lake Country that includes Magnet Hill, a ninety-million-year-old meteorite, and claims of UFO sights. Medicinal to mysterious, Lake Country is all that and more.

South central Oklahoma is a getaway filled with a treasure chest of opportunities, whether your visit is a day trip or a weekend escape. There's no question that diving into Lake Country is invigorating.

A Snip off the Old Lock

Ardmore

One day a young man stopped by Mitchell's Barber Shop in Ardmore wanting a "shag" haircut. Being unfamiliar with that style of hairdo didn't stop barber Marshall Mitchell from accepting the client. Armed with a comb in one hand and shears in the other, Marshall began clipping. He snipped this way and that way, until some time had passed and he finally decided he had accomplished the request. When Marshall whirled the old-fashioned, maroon barber chair around to face the mirror, the young man asked with a puzzled look on his face: "Is that a shag?" "Well, it looks pretty shaggy to me," Marshall replied.

Barber Marshall Mitchell gives a buzz cut to a regular customer.

Years later, Marshall boasts that he must have done a good job, because the young man never came back to have his hair redone.

Marshall and his brother, Larry, have operated the old-fashioned barbershop for more than thirty years at 540 12th Ave. NW. The interior hasn't changed over the years; a mixture of old family photos, political posters, license plates, and other trinkets decorate the walls. There are also antique telephones, an old dial-tuned television, and seating in front of the large picture window.

The two men, both in their sixties, have perfected their one and only style of cut—the "basic haircut," as well as their witty bantering that starts the instant the first customer arrives. It is usually the customer who unintentionally becomes the straight man for a jovial round of wisecracking punch lines from the brothers. Their entertaining personalities and, of course, the consistency of their one style of buzz haircut has turned many first-time customers into longtime regulars.

Larry said he had a fellow stop by one time to get a haircut while he was in town visiting relatives. He said when he was finished, the man raved about the cut.

"The fellow came back several years later, sat in my chair, and I cut his hair again. He told me he was amazed and very pleased with my memory because I cut his hair the exact same way as last time," Larry said. "Not sure the old boy knew that was the only style we do."

The brothers charge only seven dollars for their haircuts. They note that the jokes are free. Both men were trained at barber colleges. Marshall said they became barbers because they were "too lazy to work and too nervous to be still." It's an old-fashioned barbershop that used to give shaves, but all the fancy razors stopped that, Marshall said

Larry said he initially wanted to be an undertaker, "but I couldn't pass the test. I couldn't look sad at a $10,000 funeral." He added that the dead are his best customers, "no matter how bad I mess up, they never complain." Mitchell's Barber Shop takes walk-ins. Call (580) 223-2148 for shop hours.

A Pink State of Mind

Ardmore

When Heidi Chapman decided to quit her fifteen-year career as a drug and alcohol counselor to open the Cloverleaf boutique in Ardmore, some thought maybe she was under the influence and not thinking too clearly.

Maybe it is the flamboyantly pink exterior of her building, the pink bicycles outlining her parking lot, or the rather large and unusual flea-market-type items decorating her entrance that had folks around town leery. Or just maybe it's the pink wigs and boas Chapman and her employees occasionally don to emphasize how the right attitude can make for some spirited shopping.

"I'm totally in the wrong place for this kind of store," Chapman said about the conservative town of Ardmore. "Thank God the business is next to the highway, or I probably would have no business."

The Cloverleaf, an eclectic boutique, draws out-of-town shoppers.

More than 95 percent of Chapman's business is from travelers on Interstate 35 who see the rather large shop's intriguing exterior and stop. It is located at 3218 West Broadway and can be seen from I-35.

If you're attracted to the outside, you will be mesmerized by the inside and the wide array of eclectic items. It is the shop where you can find a gift for the person who has everything. It is a store you would more likely find in Austin or San Francisco. So, why open it in Ardmore? Chapman says her husband is a physician and was transferred here. It is unlikely they are leaving, and she wasn't going to let conservatism stop her.

Chapman says when she first began converting the old Cloverleaf lounge into a boutique, it was rumored she was opening an adult bookstore.

"I'm not quite sure why they thought that, but [that] first round of shoppers took one step inside and immediately turned and exited," she said rolling her eyes.

The Cloverleaf keeps shoppers browsing for hours.

The store is full of fun and quirky items, ranging from the pink wigs and slip skirts to gourmet dog treats. There are beauty products, hilariously naughty greeting cards, and funky clothes. The store also is full of reminders on the benefits of thinking pink. Chapman swears pink is not just a color, but an attitude that she lives by daily. GOT PINK? one sign asks. Next time you feel the blues coming on, go to the Cloverleaf to get into a pink state of mind.

The Cloverleaf is open seven days a week. For more information call (580) 224-0400.

Who Needs Barbie and Ken When You Have Martha and George?
Ardmore

Eliza Cruce Hall took her dolls to the Ardmore Public Library for show and tell on her birthday in 1971. A few weeks later while taking a nap, she died but not without knowing her dolls, all three hundred of them, would be forever cared for. What she may have not known was they would have their own life-size dollhouse called the Eliza Cruce Hall Museum.

Hall celebrated her eightieth birthday the day she officially donated her dolls to the library during a dedication ceremony that drew the attention of U.S. House Speaker Carl Albert, the Oklahoma Historical Society, and even the Smithsonian Institution. Hall's one-hundred-thousand-dollar collection drew more than a thousand visitors the first month it was displayed in its own section of the library, later named the Eliza Cruce Hall Museum. The dolls, some of which date back to the mid-1700s, are arranged in mirrored-backed glass display cabinets that provide a nearly 360-degree view of them.

Hall bought her first collectable doll when she was forty-five while on a trip to Europe to watch the coronation of Great Britain's George VI.

She had a life-long love of dolls and an appreciation of the art of doll making and the role dolls played throughout history. Hall claimed a group of her rare historic French dolls, carved out of wood, originally belonged to Marie Antoinette. Unfortunately, the Ardmore Public Library, which now owns three of the seven "Court Dolls," could not document the claim.

The collection also includes two English peddler dolls, circa 1830, and a Queen Anne doll, circa 1710. Other rare dolls in the collection include dolls that represent Martha and George Washington and seven "fashion dolls" made in 1860, the precursor to the mannequins of today. The fashion dolls were sent from around the world to represent the latest styles of the season.

The Eliza Cruce Hall doll collection.

The collection has many ethnic dolls from around the world, such as Kewpie dolls, baby dolls, wooden dolls, cloth dolls, and porcelain dolls. There are also miniature tea sets made from materials ranging from solid gold to Dresden and Sevres porcelains.

Hall reportedly always wanted to share her vast doll collection; she just didn't know how to do it. That is when she decided to donate the dolls to the library.

The museum is located in the Ardmore Library at 320 East Street Northwest. For more information call (580) 223-8290.

Political Clout
Near Ardmore

The largest meteorite of its kind and the fifth largest in the world lies inside Tucker Tower perched atop the precipitous outcrop called Devil's Kitchen Conglomerate at Lake Murray State Park south of Ardmore. The rock that dropped from outer space is a ninety-million-year-old granular hexahedrite meteorite. It was cut in half at the Institute of Meteorites in New Mexico allowing for a rare glimpse into its core. The meteorite was discovered during the construction of the man-made lake and park in the 1930s. Had it not been for former Gov. William H. "Alfalfa Bill" Murray, there would be no lake, no park, and no tower, and who knows whether anyone would have found the meteorite. Actually, had it not been for New Deal and Works Progress Administration projects, Governor Murray's efforts to land Oklahoma's first, and still largest, public park wouldn't have happened, at least not during his term.

Governor Murray was one of Oklahoma's more colorful politicians, known for his excessive use of executive orders, martial law, and his opposition to New Deal programs established to offset the Great

Depression. Some say his opposition to the federal programs was really just retaliation for losing the 1932 Democratic presidential nomination to Franklin D. Roosevelt. While the governor spent a lot of his time trying to thwart many of the New Deal programs, he left alone the one that allowed for the construction of the lake and tower in 1933. Perhaps he saw the worthiness of providing public recreation or liked the thought of having a castle-looking lake home. There are conflicting stories, but some say the tower was originally designed as the governor's summer retreat as appreciation for his efforts to get the lake located in southern Oklahoma. The tower was based on pictures of European castles taken by World War I veteran and then local legislator Fred Tucker.

The largest meteor of its kind lies inside Tucker Tower.

The tower is 65 feet tall and provides a spectacular view of the lake. It is reported that a cave that lies beneath the tower and water was once inhabited by an earlier culture and in later years by outlaws hiding out. The meteorite is just one of the fascinating items that can be found at Tucker Tower. There is much hidden there, providing an unbelievable experience for naturalists and inquisitive sorts. The tower is open from Memorial Day to Labor Day. It is closed December and January. For more information call (580) 223-2109.

Hammer Out a Good Time
Bennington

The Annual Master Works Sawdust Festival held in the tiny southern town of Bennington draws folks from across the country for a weekend of jamming, eating, and fellowship. Don't be fooled by the festival's title; there are no fiddles or steel guitars or any guitar being played at this weekend gig. The featured instrument is the hammer dulcimer and an occasional bowed psaltery. Huh? Never heard of it? Well, not to worry; there are many of us who are musically challenged.

The festival, founded by Russell Cook who makes the ancient instrument, is held the last weekend in September. The event attracts some of the best dulcimer players in the country, who jam and hold workshops. It's a family-oriented musical experience, where beginners can learn from the best.

The dulcimer, which is struck with hammers, is a member of the zither family. The instrument originated in Persia about A.D. 1000 and by the fifteenth century was very popular in Europe and in the Far East by the eighteenth century. In recent times, they're often heard in mountain music, folk songs, and Celtic tunes. They are also featured at Renaissance fairs. Regardless of your musical knowledge, the sound emitted from a hammer dulcimer is magical with a charm that can convert just about anyone.

That charm captivated Cook, a former science teacher, nearly thirty years ago while playing around on a dulcimer made from a kit his brother-in-law bought. The fascination drove him to build his own dulcimer in 1979 out of an old junk piano he found under a big oak tree while driving a school bus one day. Cook then taught himself how to play the instrument, and by 1981 he had won first place at the Southern Regional Dulcimer Competition.

That same year, Cook quit teaching and opened a business in which he built about a thousand instruments during the 1980s. By the end of 2006, Cook's business had made seventy-three hundred hammer dulcimers and about a thousand bowed psalteries. Cook, assisted by Pheyland Barthen, makes the handcrafted instruments at his company, Master Works, in Bennington.

For more information about the Annual Master Works Sawdust Festival, visit www.masterworksok.com or call (580) 847-2273.

Pheyland Barthen demonstrates how to use a bow on a handcrafted dulcimer.

KISS OF DEATH

It doesn't seem likely that controversy would surround the choosing of the state's official flower, but controversy abounds in Oklahoma's flower choice. Up until 2004, the state's flower was not a flower at all, but a poisonous semiparasitic plant, the mistletoe.

Legend has it that the mistletoe was the only winter plant available to decorate the grave of an early settler's wife who died during a winter influenza epidemic in the 1890s. A friend of the couple vowed that if Oklahoma ever became a state he would see to it that the mistletoe became the state flower in memory of the wife. Whether true or not, the story was part of Oklahoma's school history books explaining why in 1893 the Territorial Legislature adopted the mistletoe as the state flower. So, when statehood finally came in 1907, so did the mistletoe.

Despite the mistletoe's popular tradition of encouraging kissing under its greenery, the criticism of having a deadly parasitic plant that grows in trees high on branches as the state flower continued for decades.

So, in order to have a flower that was indeed a flower, the state made the Oklahoma Rose its official flower in 2004, and changed the mistletoe to its official state floral emblem. Most Okies, however, will argue that the mistletoe is still the state flower.

LAKE COUNTRY

Say a Little Prayer

Dickson

Just outside the little community of Dickson is the Tiny Chapel with its tiny altar and tiny pews. Mr. Trible built the chapel, according to a framed thank-you letter that is hanging in the one-person sized lobby. It appears he constructed the red chapel with a white steeple as a memorial to his sons who preceded him in death.

The chapel isn't one of those tourist sites placed in plain sight along the highway with a huge neon sign and gift shop luring travelers to stop. Instead, it's tucked a few miles off Highway 199 on a dirt road, all alone in the solitude of God's country. A driver can easily miss the small sign directing the turn off the highway onto Durwood Street.

Once you leave the highway, there are only a couple of even smaller signs attached to barbed-wire fencing to help guide you there. About the time some motorist might seek assistance from a higher power, the Tiny Chapel appears from out of nowhere.

The trek apparently hasn't discouraged too many; a spiral notebook in the lobby is nearly filled with dated inspirational thoughts from visitors, who have traveled there from across the country. Several framed notes and tributes hang on the walls. Beyond the

The Tiny Chapel holds six two-seater pews and a tiny altar.

lobby is the chapel that for some people is no bigger than an oversized walk-in closet.

Inside the semi-darkened chapel are four faux stained-glass windows, two on each side and six pews each big enough for two children or two very slim adults. The only thing that appears oversized is the Bible, or at least it looks oversized considering its surroundings. Fully entering the chapel requires the door to be closed. A latch on the door triggers soft lighting to illuminate the altar and recorded old-time Gospel music to play through hidden speakers.

Anyone who wants the privacy of a spiritual moment in a traditional setting where singing hymnals out of tune goes unnoticed and Bible readings are of one's own choosing, the Tiny Chapel may be your heavenly place.

What a Goober
Durant

The small city of Durant in southern Oklahoma was once home to a peanut industry that claimed to be one of the largest in the state. So large that in later years, long after the industry had died out, townsfolk decided to pay homage to the shelled seed that helped keep this town thriving. Hence, the town's rendition of the World's Largest Peanut, which sits atop of a monument in front of City Hall.

Now, if this peanut depicted the true size of one that actually existed, Durant would have something extremely unique. But since it doesn't, the approximately 3-foot-long peanut touted to be the world's largest seems kind of nuts, since Ashburn, Georgia, has a 10-foot tall Goober Goliath and Persall, Texas, has one 6 feet tall.

Not many at Durant's City Hall can tell you why the peanut got tagged the supreme kernel of all peanuts and are quick to tell you about the larger ones in Georgia and Texas. The monument on which the peanut sits states that it is a dedication to the Bryan County Peanut Growers and Processors, November 15, 1974. City officials say Durant was once one of the largest peanut farming communities in this part of the state but stop short of claiming any worldwide status.

Stopping in Durant to take a look-see or a snapshot of the revered peanut is worth your while if you're already traveling nearby. The peanut may not be all that it's cracked up to be, but that doesn't mean there is anything nutty about a small town that thinks big.

The nut is located outside City Hall at 300 West Evergreen Street.

WORLD'S LARGEST
PEANUT

DEDICATED TO THE BRYAN COUNTY
PEANUT GROWERS AND PROCESSORS
NOV. 15, 1974

The city of Durant claims to have the world's largest peanut.

Chili Forecast
Durant

It's hard to believe that a No. 4 chili-cheeseburger at George's Drive-In would link lovers together forever, but it has.

A staple in Durant for sixty years, George's continues to be a popular burger joint with residents and a lot of the students from Southeastern Oklahoma State University.

"I can't tell you how many times older customers will tell me they drove all the way from Texas, or other parts of Oklahoma just to have one of George's chili-cheeseburgers," said owner Paul Lovan.

"I also get a lot of stories about how they met their wife or husband here while going to school at the university," he said.

Owner Paul Lovan flips burgers at George's Drive-in, a city landmark.

LAKE COUNTRY

The popular eating spot, built in the 1940s, serves nine official drive-up spots. It was originally called Pete's, before George Bryant bought it in the mid-1950s. Lovan purchased it a few years back and decided to keep the name and hopefully the thriving business. His decision panned out. Word-of-mouth has been the best advertisement for George's, particularly among students attending Southeastern Oklahoma State University, located near the burger stand. Lovan said people drive here to have lunch or dinner from all over the place, including from neighboring states.

The secret to his success and ability to compete with Sonic and Dairy Queen, both close by, is his ingredients—everything is fresh daily.

Potatoes for the french fries are peeled and cut every day. The business goes through about nine hundred pounds of potatoes a week, he said. All of the produce is fresh and prepared each day. George's used to buy its beef locally, but a change in the economy forced the restaurant to purchase it from the U.S. Department of Agriculture. One of the key ingredients is the chili, made from a sixty-year-old recipe. The chili-cheeseburger and the chili coney are extremely popular.

George's isn't fancy, nor does it have any gimmick to lure you—it's all about tradition, good food, and dependability, some of the same qualities that makes for a good marriage.

George's Drive-In is located at 1301 North First Street. It's open Monday through Saturday.

Plowing through Time

Murray County

Jim Dyer has plowed through every kind of antique tractor you can imagine. When he finds one that needs fixing, he can't help but buy it. He has been collecting these machines that revolutionized the agriculture industry for quite some time. His oldest is from 1919 and it runs on kerosene. His newest is a 1950 model that operates on gasoline.

Dyer is a former editor of an agriculture magazine, who now devotes all of his time to refurbishing tractors and attending tractor shows. Talking to him about his tractor collection is definitely a conversation for the mechanically inclined. But, viewing the antique tractors is quite appealing to everyone whether you know what an internal combustion engine or a horizontal cross engine is or not. The tractors are just cool to look at.

Jim Dyer shows the 1916 Frick "Eclipse" steam engine tractor.

Dyer is a member of the Murray County Antique Tractor and Implement Association, one of several tractor clubs in the state. The club, located between Sulphur and Pauls Valley, houses many of the members' tractors, which are on display year-round by appointment. On a walk through the tractor grounds, Dyer points out the 1916 Frick "Eclipse" steam engine that has a coal-fired boiler. Then there is the 1920 Rumely "Oil Pull" tractor that has a huge crank bar. He says these two are some of the more popular among visitors.

The 1919 Fordson is a tractor that a lot of collectors have because so many were made. Henry Ford & Son made the Fordson, many of which were used in World War I, Dyer says. Fordson made the tractors in quantity and sold them cheap, he says. The tractors aren't that efficient. They're hard to stop and at times tip backward, but because of the price everyone had one, Dyer said.

Besides the tractor collection, Dyer boasts about the association's devotion to the education of early farming. The group holds a show annually the third weekend in September that has races and farming demonstrations using the old tractors. Proceeds are going to complete an antique tractor and implement museum on the association's sixty-acre grounds.

Anyone who is fascinated with tractors or who just likes looking at fun antiques should visit the Murray County Antique Tractor and Implement Association. Dyer can be contacted at (580) 465-3265 or visit www.arbuckletourism.com/mcatia.

Superheroes
Pauls Valley

The world's only Toy & Action Figure Museum in Pauls Valley appeals to everyone because it unleashes the inner child. No matter how cranky or old a person is as an adult, everyone had a favorite toy when they were young, and this museum taps into those memories.

But unlike most museums where you can't touch anything, here children are allowed to play with many of the toys, says curator Kevin Stark, a local artist who designed the Teenage Mutant Turtles and the

The Toy & Action Figure Museum has thousands of toys, many of which visitors can touch.

Toxic Crusaders figurines. The interactive nature of the museum was an important principle when the community decided to convert a 6,000-square-foot abandoned department store into a haven of action figures toys, a distinction that separates it from other toy museums, Stark said.

"We thought is would be torturous for four and five year olds to come to a museum full of toys and not be able to play with anything," he said.

The museum does have a few of the toys out of reach and still in the original packaging, like the first action figure from Hasbro, the original 12-inch-tall GI Joe. The museum also has the original Spawn line from McFarlane Toys.

Other figures found in the enormous collection are the big names, like Superman, Spider-Man, Batman the caped crusader, who has an entire cave dedicated to him, and of course, Robin and some of their foes. There are also easily recognized figures, like the Hulk, Luke Skywalker, Bart Simpson, and Mickey Mouse. An older crowd might gravitate to Captain Marvel, the robot from *Lost in Space*, Zorro, and the little green army figures that have waged many a war on the lawns of houses across America. There are more than seven thousand figures in the museum. The population of Pauls Valley is only sixty-three hundred.

Stark donated much of his own personal collection to get the nonprofit museum off the ground, and the museum has received donations since the doors opened in 2005. The museum also features Oklahoman cartoonists and comics and offers a Lego room and an area where kids can dress up in superhero costumes.

The museum, located at 111 South Chickasaw Street, is open 10:00 a.m. to 5.00 p.m. Tuesday through Saturday and 1:00 to 5:00 p.m. on Sunday. For more details visit www.actionfiguremuseum.com or call (405) 238-6300.

Everything's Golden
Ringling

When members of the Wade family vowed on their wedding day "til death do us part," they meant it. And for fifty years, that promise rang true in this large family that was reared on a farm in the small town of Ringling. The nuptial devotion of the six sisters and six brothers earned their family a Guinness Book World Record in 2005 for having the greatest number of siblings to reach their golden marker of marital bliss.

"O.K., maybe not bliss, but close to it," Drue Wade Patrick said with a smile.

"I reckon sticking to our faith, our community, and each other is all we know. We learned that from our hardworking, Christian parents who stuck to their principles and taught us the gift of forgiveness. So, nobody stays mad too long."

Today, just making it through the "seven-year itch," is a feat many married couples rave about. Yes, Alice and Charley Wade, the proud parents of these dedicated couples, set the example. They were married for sixty-four years until Charley died at age ninety-one. Alice later died at age one hundred.

"It was actually my [older] sister, Beuhla, who realized we probably had the record. She called me after reading an article about a Texas family that had held the record with 11 siblings. She said, 'Drue, we have them beat. I think we might hold the record.' "

Drue said Beulah died in 2001 at age eighty-six before she had a chance to find out whether Beulah was right. Drue, along with her twin sister, Ella, is seventy-six, and the youngest of the siblings.

"She depended on me to do it, so I called on the family and we began," Drue said.

The effort took nearly a year to complete because birth, marriage, and death certificates were needed to prove the claim. For most people, that wouldn't be problematic, but for births that occurred in a farmhouse in the early 1900s, the task is a little more challenging. Some of the documentation, Patrick said, included pictures of tombstones and affidavits from townsfolk, including one from the only woman left living in Ringling that could vouch "momma" and "papa" Wade were married, she said.

To learn more about the Wade family, go to Ringling and ask anybody. If they're not a Wade, they'll know where to find one.

Drue Wade Patrick shows off her Guiness World Record.

The Greatest Show on Earth Just Went South

Ringling

Circus operator John Ringling founded the rural town of Ringling in 1914 to house his traveling circus. He was instrumental in having a railroad track extended west from Ardmore to Ringling for just that reason. But, then he realized the winters were sporadic and could get too cold for his crew and his audience, so in 1927 he packed up the tents, performers, and animals and relocated his winter headquarters to Saratoga, Florida, leaving behind those who were determined to keep the town alive. The struggle was hard with the absence of the circus, and while many eventually left, the town still exists. It has a school and a small downtown area with a bank, a newspaper office, a post office, and a few shops like a dry goods store. Some of the townsfolk reminisce about watching the circus staff practice their performances. The town may not be under the Big Top any more, but faded signs on either side of town still reminds travelers that it once was home to the Greatest Show on Earth.

Being Pulled in the Wrong Direction

Springer

The area around Springer in southern Oklahoma is known for supernatural events such as UFO sightings in Ardmore and meteorites dropping into Lake Murray. So, when a magnetic hill was discovered outside of Springer, the locals didn't seem to be too awed by it. Sure, it is a place to take visitors, since there isn't anything else to do unless you trek south to Ardmore or north to Pauls Valley.

Nobody knows who discovered the mysterious hill on Pioneer Road about a mile off Highway 53, west of Interstate 35. Magnet hill is just what is sounds like—a magnet. Seeing what happens to a car left at the bottom of the road in neutral with the brakes released is all it takes to make a visitor a believer. It takes only a few seconds and then it begins. As God is my witness, my 2004 Camry rolled backward uphill, at speeds of up to 15 mph. Trying it again, but with the car facing forward up the hill, didn't seem to work like it did going backward.

Pioneer Road is only about one-half mile long. When you turn off Highway 53 onto Pioneer Road headed north, it's not long before the blacktop road disappears, indicating you are about to top a hill. The road is more long than steep and at the bottom, about 10 yards from where it meets up with Vermont Road, there are patches of gravel that have settled in the middle of it, an obvious indicator you've reached the bottom of the hill.

Magnet hill definitely must be experienced to be believed.

A vehicle is moving backward up a slight hill on Pioneer Road outside of Springer.

A Drink for the Well-To-Do

Sulphur

Sulphur, located near the Arbuckle Mountains, is home to the largest artesian well in Oklahoma, the Vendome Well. The mineral water that shoots up from the well into the air at least 10 feet is said to have medicinal qualities.

"Once you get used to the rotten egg smell and taste, it's not that bad," said Louis Milsap, who drives down every two weeks from Oklahoma City to replenish his supply. Milsap has several plastic milk containers that he fills up. The elderly man says he swears by the mineral water.

"It helps my aches. It keeps me healthy," he said as he paused from filling his containers to watch a few boys roustabout in the water.

Milsap isn't the only one to rely on the mineral water for medicinal purposes. The indigenous people of the southern plain, settlers, and others have treasured Sulphur and its abundance of sulfur wells. The area is known for its healing waters.

The area became the first national park in the state shortly after the turn of the twentieth century, when Chickasaws ceded it and the thirty different wells to the government to prevent it from being destroyed by development. The park has changed names in the past but is now called the Chickasaw National Recreation Area.

In the early days, "mud puppies" were a common sight in the park. Visitors would cover themselves with mud and dry in the sun along the Vendome stream. The mud puppies believed the black sticky mud along the stream banks contained medicinal properties that would heal skin problems and arthritis. By the 1920s, bathhouses were opening near the park, providing patrons endless hours to spend soaking in the tubs full of sulphur water.

It is estimated that the park has 3.4 million visitors a year making it one of the most visited for its size in the entire national park system, according to park reports. The park has diverse natural resources, nature trails, campgrounds, a nature center, and numerous natural springs in which to swim, including those like Vendome that produce mineral water.

Although many are convinced of the healing properties of the water, the park makes it clear it "neither substantiates or denies" claims that the water has medicinal value.

The park, located at 1008 West Second Street in Sulphur, is free. It is closed Christmas and New Year's Day.

This mineral water is good for the body and the soul.

Catch of the Day
Tishomingo

Oklahoma noodling has absolutely nothing to do with making pasta, unless you count the use of your bare hands. It does, however, have to do with food, sort of. It's a fishing method in which some Okies try to capture their catch of the day without the catch capturing them. This art of hand fishing for enormous flathead catfish is a sport not without risk. It originally began as a food-gathering technique of the American Indians, but it has evolved into a popular sport mostly among rural men, whose average age is about forty, research shows.

The sport is so popular in Oklahoma that there are annual summer noodling tournaments, like the June National Noodling Tournament and Festival in Tishomingo and the longstanding July Okie Catfish Noodling Tournament in Pauls Valley.

These country anglers come from across the region to noodle and are easily spotted sporting the official noodling uniform—bare chest, denim cut-offs, tattered water slippers, and of course, the ever-popular mullet hairdo if they have hair at all. These serious noodlers are willing to give up some blood and risk death. Those noodlers who resort to underwater apparatuses like snorkels and scuba gear are not real hand fishers, some will argue. Many tournaments bar those devices. It's man versus water creature. Earning the title for bringing in the heaviest flat-head "cat" far outweighs the prize money for nearly all of the participants.

These noodlers dive beneath the water scouring the banks and river bottom for underwater burrows. They then probe and prod the holes searching for flathead catfish to take the bait—their hand. Once the sharp, toothy jaws of the cat clamps the hand, an underwater battle ensues as the noodler wrestles his catch to the surface, wrapping his legs around the more than 50-pound fish as it fiercely rolls like a gator trying to drown its prey. Most noodling is practiced with at least two anglers to ensure safety. There are times when a noodler reaches in a hole to find a snapping turtle, a pit of snakes, or even a beaver. None of those scenarios have a pleasant ending.

Suspicion of cheating is always raised if a noodler comes to weigh in his catch without bloody knuckles and forearms. All noodlers are told up front that they are subject to polygraph tests. These anglers are serious about the sport in its rawest form.

In *Webster's* unabridged dictionary, noodling is defined as "a fool." Now, isn't that interesting considering the sport? So, maybe French novelist Sidonie-Gabrielle Colette has a point when she said: "You will do foolish things, but do them with enthusiasm." And there is no arguing, these noodlers do just that.

The National Noodling Tournament and Festival in Tishomingo is held in late June. Call (580) 371-2175 for more information on the dates. The Okie Catfish Noodling Tournament in Pauls Valley is held in early July. For more information on dates, contact (405) 238-2332.

Mark McFarland of Enid (left) and Billy Curtis of Blackwell (right) pull up two catfish during the National Noodling Tournament.

BITE FIGHTS

When boxer Mike Tyson bit off a piece of Evander Holyfield's ear during a match in 1997, it was hard to believe because it was so bizarre. Oklahoma had its own little wave of biting incidents for five consecutive months from December 2005 to April 2006. Then as quickly and strangely as the biting started, it stopped.

December 2005

A sixteen-year-old Chickasha boy and his twenty-one-year-old brother were fighting when their mother decided to step in between the boys to break it up. When she did, the younger boy latched on to his mother's bottom lip with his teeth and proceeded to bite it off. The woman's lip was so mangled doctors were unable to reattach it, according to news accounts.

New Year's Eve 2005

An altercation between two Enid men ended with one biting off a huge chunk of the other's ear. When the police caught up with the biter, he admitted to the ear-munching incident. Not only was the biter arrested, but his wife was also reportedly arrested for assaulting her husband. Apparently, when she found out about her husband's biting incident, she beat the snot out of him. There were never any charges filed against the couple.

January 2006

A Panama man, who came to the rescue of a woman being assaulted by a twenty-one-year-old hoodlum, got a portion of his ear bitten off. The hoodlum was charged with two counts of assault.

February 2006

A former Tulsa woman and her boyfriend were visiting family in Tulsa. The family had just sat down for supper when the woman came out of a bedroom with a bloody towel pressed to her face. Her boyfriend had bitten her nose off.

The boyfriend was arrested not only for assault and battery, but also for destroying evidence—he had swallowed her nose.

April 2006

The same hoodlum who bit off a man's ear in January bit off the index finger of another good Samaritan who was breaking up a fight between the hoodlum and his younger brother. The Samaritan, now with one less finger, began defending himself and, perhaps fearing the loss of another finger, proceeded to kick the hoodlum in the face. That's one method of disarming a biter—knock out his teeth.

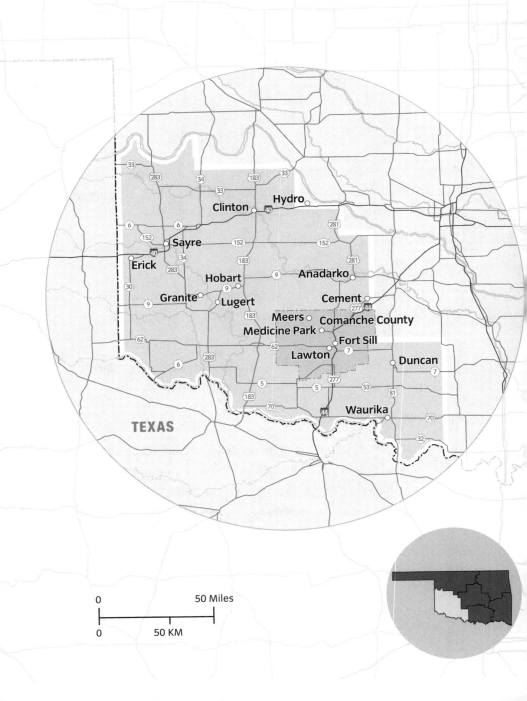

GREAT PLAINS COUNTRY

Clinton
Hydro
Sayre
Erick
Hobart
Granite
Lugert
Anadarko
Cement
Meers
Comanche County
Medicine Park
Fort Sill
Lawton
Duncan
Waurika

TEXAS

0   50 Miles
0   50 KM

GREAT PLAINS COUNTRY

Route 66, from Illinois to California, was dubbed "the Mother Road" in *The Grapes of Wrath* by John Steinbeck, who chose this route for his fictional Joad family to escape the dust bowl in Oklahoma and travel to the "land of milk and honey" in California. Not only does the Oklahoma Great Plains Country offer the mother road, it also hands over the mother lode for the total number of "Main Street of America" miles that Oklahoma has within its borders. Because it contains more of Route 66 than any other state, Oklahoma is home to the Route 66 Museum, located in Clinton (Not to be confused with the National Route 66 Museum featured on page 186).

If driving cattle is how you get your kicks, you can beef up your visit to the Great Plains Country and visit another famous byway that this part of Oklahoma offers: the Chisholm Trail, the old cattle trail that cut through Oklahoma to get to the Kansas railways. Visit the Chisholm Trail Heritage Center in Duncan and experience what it felt like to drive thousands of head of cattle long before the days of semitrucks.

The Great Plains of Oklahoma also gives its visitors natural beauty in the magnificent mountain ranges, numerous lakes, stunning prairies, and the famous plains it is named for. Along with the natural landscape come the critters that inhabit it. From the abundant rattlesnakes in the Waurika area to the plentiful prairie dogs in Lawton, Great Plains Country is home to numerous wild animals—and wild people, both past and present. Read on and see for yourself what a great time can be had in the Great Plains of Oklahoma.

History Stamped in the Post Office

Anadarko

Murals decorating the walls of a U.S. post office may not be that big of a deal. But when the murals are seventy years old and the artist's commission is the largest ever awarded to a Southern Plains Indian artist, the perspective changes.

The late Stephen Mopope, one of the original Kiowa Five artists, depicted the ceremony and social life of the Kiowas in sixteen mural panels on the walls of the Anadarko Post Office.

One mural, *The Deer Hunter,* is a painting of a hunter that has a successful hunt despite the scarcity of game and the grueling trek. There are three murals showing the tribe preparing for the winter migration south. Five murals show the importance of the buffalo, signifying health and food for all.

The U.S. Post Office in Anadarko depicts the life of Kiowa Indians.

The mural *The Men in Council* honors the sun dance, a ceremony held each summer prior to buffalo hunts. An accomplished dancer himself, Mopope painted seven other murals symbolizing various dance ceremonies.

Mopope used brilliant colors of tempera paint in the murals. In 1990 Justin James Jones, a monk at St. Gregory's Abbey in Shawnee, restored the painting with funding from the Leslie Powell Foundation and the Kirkpatrick Foundation.

Walls of post offices built in the Great Depression era throughout the country have murals reflecting America's history. Most of those, however, need to be restored or have since vanished.

Excuse Me, What Did You Say Your Name Is?
Cement

A mistake by a postal worker cemented the name of this small town as Cement, rather than its intended name of Acme. In 1901 a group of businessmen decided to take advantage of the pure, baby-powder-fine gypsum sulfate that could be found naturally just outside of town. They built the Acme Cement mill and then hauled the gypsum sulfate to the mill, mixed it with horsehair, bagged the mixture, and shipped it by rail to Chicago and New York City. It was quite a successful venture.

The community began to grow, and the leaders decided they wanted Acme to officially become a town but needed to establish a post office to do it. Oklahoma wasn't a state yet and the only way to get a post office was to have an existing post office make application for it. The group sought the assistance of a post office in a little town called Keechi, which agreed to make the application. When it came time to fill out the paperwork, the postal worker in Keechi couldn't remember the name of the community. All he could remember is that it was built around a cement mill. So, instead of becoming Acme, the town officially became Cement. The name hardened so quickly that apparently nobody took time to try to change it. This small town can be found in Caddo County just southeast of Chickasha.

In an attempt to beautify the town, Cement erected a donated Statue of Liberty streetlight.

Heartbreak Hotel

Clinton

People from around the world come to Clinton to spend the night in room 215 at the Best Western Trade Winds Inn on Route 66. With crushed red velvet full-length window drapes and a red satin bedspread over the king bed, it is the only room at the motel that hasn't changed in more than thirty years. There are two 1960s retro white Naugahyde chairs that frame a small table and a black Naugahyde, S-curved daybed. The gaudy furnishings are straight out of a Las Vegas lounge. The room screams Elvis Presley, and that's because the King slept there—four times on his travels between Las Vegas and Memphis.

"I've shown the Elvis Suite more than one hundred times," said Mary Jernigan, a housekeeper who has worked at the motel for thirty-four years. She started working a couple years after Elvis made his last visit.

Elvis slept here.

"I can tell you all about it. I know a lot about Elvis. I've been in love with him since I was a teenager," she said.

Jernigan said during Elvis's glory days, he and his entourage would travel by bus down Route 66. The King chose Clinton because it was a good stopping point that would break up the roadtrip. Room 215 was situated away from the street, somewhat secluded, and each time Elvis stopped he asked for the same room, which was furnished in a style that was a perfect fit for the King of Rock 'n' Roll who often played Las Vegas.

Elvis and his entourage would arrive about midnight and sleep most of the next day and then leave late in the evening. Elvis never left the room. He ordered meals from room service.

Then on one of his visits in 1972, a motel employee delivering his meal recognized Elvis and went through town like Paul Revere alerting everybody, Jernigan said. In no time a huge crowd had gathered in the parking lot outside his room. Although Elvis graciously came out and spoke with the crowd and even tossed a ball around with some of the local boys, it was an event that would later break the townspeople's hearts. For that was the last sighting of Elvis in Clinton. When he left town that night, he never returned—likely due to the unsolicited fanfare. That didn't stop the motel, however, from capitalizing on its most famous patron; it kept room 215 intact over the decades, knowing it could offer something only a few other motels could—an opportunity to sleep in Elvis's bed.

The Best Western Trade Winds Inn is located at 2128 Gary Boulevard (also Route 66) just west of town. A night in the Elvis Suite comes with a certificate. For more information on the room and rates, call (405) 323-2610.

Holy Moley What a Crowd
Comanche County

Holy City is an outdoor theater located in the hilly terrain of the Wichita Mountains Wildlife Refuge. It is a natural amphitheater created for what has become the country's longest-running passion play, *The Prince of Peace*.

Jessica Powell stands next to her sister Bethany in Herod's Court at Holy City.

Holy City is the brainchild of Methodist reverend Anthony Wallock, who fell in love with the grandeur of the wildlife refuge during his first visit. The place reminded him of the Holy Land. In 1926 he started gathering a small group of people from his church and Sunday school class for a hillside Easter service that included scripture, song, and a pantomime of Jesus's life. The short, early morning service was the birth of the annual Easter pageant, *The Prince of Peace*.

The success of the service quickly grew, attracting six thousand spectators by 1931 and fifteen thousand the following year. By then the cast numbered 150. By 1934 the attendance was forty thousand. The popularity helped Wallock get a grant specifically to construct a full-scale replica of the Holy City for the Easter pageant. The first set of buildings was completed in March 1935 and that April the pageant drew an audience of eighty-two thousand. The following year, a telegram from President Franklin D. Roosevelt was read during a radio broadcast of the pageant. There were two thousand cast members and a hundred thousand in attendance from sixty-five cities.

The first set of buildings included Calvary's Mount, the Temple Court, Pilate's Judgment Hall, Watch Towers, the Garden of Gethsemane, dressing rooms, and rock shrines. Then a few years later, additions included the Lord's Supper Building, Herod's Court, a lodge, and a control room. Also constructed were the Chapel of the Holy City, reminiscent of an old world temple with wood carvings, and biblical murals in the interior.

The 1948 movie *The Lawton Story—The Prince of Peace* was filmed at the site.

In the early years, the pageant was a sunrise passion play and timed to end at dawn. By 1986 the time had changed twice and now the play begins at 9 p.m. on Easter eve. Tourists from across the country and abroad visit the Holy City. Overlooking the city is an 11-foot-tall white marble statue of Christ that was erected in 1975. The refuge is open year-round and located just west of Medicine Park off Oklahoma 49.

Action Flick
Duncan

There is only one place in the country where you can experience a cattle drive and all of its intensity without ever going outside and mounting a horse. The Chisholm Heritage Museum in Duncan has a small interactive theater that recreates a cattle drive using cutting-edge technology and state-of-the-art visual and physical special effects pioneered by Universal Studios and Disney World. Opened in 2005, it's a theater that literally plays to the human senses.

The short film portrays twenty-four hours on a cattle drive, which at first blush seems corny, if not boring. But to everyone's surprise, there is nothing remotely dreary about this flick. It stimulates your mind from the start as it arouses your senses.

Colten Browning lassoes a bull in the interactive portion of the Chisholm Heritage Museum.

It's dawn and you smell the coffee brewing on the campfire. You smell the grasses in the pasture and the early stages of a storm as it begins to form. You feel the dust and heat of the day and the coolness of night. When it rains, you get wet, and when it's windy, you get blown. There is even a terrifying lightning storm that triggers a stampede, intensely stirring several senses at once, making you recoil in your seat for fear the action is going to leap off the screen. It's as good as, if not better than, some of Hollywood's action movies.

Museum officials set out specifically to provide an experience that leaves visitors wanting to return, said Bill Benson, museum executive director.

Benson said because everyone's senses are different, they experience the theater differently. He said he was initially surprised at how much the blind and deaf patrons enjoyed it. Then he realized that the other senses of people who are blind or deaf are heightened, and since the theater stimulates all the senses, they enjoy the experience too. You don't need to see the action or hear the dialogue to experience this film. Much of the sound is so dramatic that you feel the vibrations of it, Benson said.

Besides the interactive theater, the museum also offers interactive exhibits geared for children.

The museum is located at 1000 North Chisholm Trail Parkway. It is open year-round except on Easter, Thanksgiving, Christmas, and New Year's Day. For more information call (580) 252-6692 or visit www.onthechisholmtrail.com.

It's a Monumental Drive

Duncan

Standing 16 feet high and 35 feet wide, the sculpture outside the Heritage Museum in Duncan is Oklahoma's largest bronze sculpture. The statue depicts a herd of cattle driven by cowboys behind a chuck wagon, and it symbolizes life on the unforgiving, unpredictable landscape of the Chisholm Trail that stretched across Oklahoma from Texas to Kansas. Oklahoma artist Paul Moore created the sculpture in his trademark style where the images pop out in dimensional form from a flat backdrop, and it took two years to complete. Many people describe it as an "eerily realistic image" of a Chisholm Trail cattle drive. The museum is located at 1000 North Chisholm Trail Parkway.

Oklahoma's largest bronze sculpture depicts a Chisholm cattle drive.

Don't Judge a Book by Its Cover

Duncan

Tucked in a neighborhood of modest homes and groomed yards is a residence that sorely sticks out. In fact, it screams of intrigue. Is it haunted? Does a recluse live there? Or has 1101 Beech Avenue in Duncan just been abandoned?

Those daring enough to venture beyond the unruly vegetation devouring the white, New Orleans-style wrought-iron fence and arched gateway surrounding the tattered Victorian house will find a magical reward. Protected from the outside world lies a wonderful emerald blend of flora, seven hundred plant species strategically placed in a fusion of neoclassical and Victorian designed flowerbeds. Shrubs are sculptured in the European tradition. Some call it Duncan's own secret garden. However, owner Pat Homrig likens his hidden treasure more to the southern feel of the setting in *Midnight in the Garden of Good and Evil.* Cobblestone paths wind through a sanctuary of sculptured gardens, water ponds, statues, old iron lampposts, and ornate wrought-iron gazebos. Homrig's garden is a virtual kaleidoscope, slowly changing color with the seasons. While green is clearly its base coat, creating a regal foundation during color transition, spring is its crowning moment, expressing the vibrancy of a rainbow's hues.

The garden isn't the only surprise Homrig's property holds. His 1903 house is a treasure chest of antiquities, artifacts, and fine art ranging from an original oil by seventeenth-century Flemish master Peter Paul Rubens to dynastic jade and rare crystal chandeliers. Homrig, a retired art teacher and current art appraiser, was featured in *Who's Who in Art Experts.*

Homrig's home, which he has named Homrighausen's Galleries, is open to the public daily by appointment only. He claims to have had many celebrities and dignitaries visit his collection, none of whom he is willing to name.

Homrig said what he loves about his place, both inside and out, is that it is all an illusion.

"There's the outside world, a known to everyone. But inside here is a whole other world, a spectacular unknown. I like it that way."

To make an appointment for a tour of Homrig's garden and vast art collection. call (580) 255-3331.

Pat Homrig shows some of the fine crystal displayed in his home.

Swapping Tongue for Jesus?

Duncan

Every fall religious youth groups gather in Duncan for a real tongue-lashing. Many of the teens paint their faces like sports fanatics and don homemade regalia prior to entering a field, fifteen to twenty at a time, to confront what has become an annual ritual—the Ultimate Cow Tongue Tournament.

The game is played like Ultimate Frisbee but with a three-pound, one-foot-long, raw beef tongue freshly purchased from a local meat market. The rules are simple: Holding the tongue isn't allowed. You have to muscle the tongue up the field through a series of tosses until one of your teammates has caught the tongue in the end zone. Players are warned,

Members of the First Christian Church's youth group toss a beef tongue during a tongue-throwing contest.

however, that a slip of the tongue on a crucial toss can cost their team the tournament and the traveling golden cow-skull trophy.

First Christian Church youth director Bryan Peters said the tournament is the brainchild of the church's former youth director, who started it in 1997 as a means of engaging the teens. His mission was easily accomplished, and the teens are anything but tongue-tied when it comes to the holy reason they're gathered together.

Knowledge of the event has traveled by word of mouth, making it all the way to the editors of Fox Sports, who featured the 2001 tournament on a segment called, "You've Gotta See This."

Peters said the tournament is very entertaining to watch as the teens scramble to catch the slimy tongue. As the meat heats up, it can stretch up to three feet long. The only eligibility for players is that they must belong to their respective youth groups. To encourage teamwork, points in the end zone are awarded as follows: five for an end-zone toss between two guys, seven for a toss between two girls, and ten for a toss between a guy and a girl.

The winners get their name on the trophy and possession of it for a year. The losers? Well, instead of the congratulatory hand slap, the losers line up and the tongue is slapped across their cheeks for a real tongue licking.

Every fall when the religious youth of southern Oklahoma come together, one thing's for sure—it's utterly tongue-on-cheek when it comes to a spirit-filled day of fun. For more information contact the First Christian Church at (580) 255-6116.

THE MOTHER ROAD

Oklahoma has a longer stretch of Route 66 running through it than any of the seven other states that have a piece of the historic east-west highway. Of the 2,440 miles of historic pavement that once was a pulsing artery from Chicago, Illinois, to Santa Monica, California, more than 400 miles of it lie in Oklahoma. Christened "the Mother Road" by John Steinbeck in his novel, *The Grapes of Wrath*, the highway travels through three time zones, metropolitan hubs, small towns, and rural countryside.

Dedicated in 1926, the highway in Oklahoma became a road of opportunity for many during the Great Depression era and the dust-bowl migration. It was the automobile connection between the east and west. But the later construction of Interstate 40 caused a lot of Route 66 to disappear or languish from the lack of automobile traffic.

Recently, life is reviving along what is left of the highway, spawned by a nostalgic attraction to the past. The highway is drawing tourists from around the country and abroad who are hungry to recapture or just experience a piece of the Americana that the route represents.

As Oklahoma author and expert on the highway Michael Wallis notes, "the spirit of Route 66 is purring along like a vintage Corvette engine. The interest in Route 66—not only here but all around the world—is growing. It's just amazing."

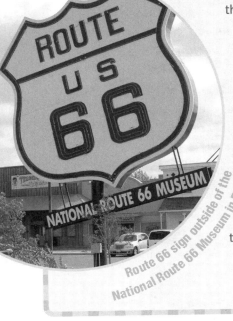

Route 66 sign outside of the National Route 66 Museum in Elk City.

Redneck Jam
Erick

The SandHills Curiosity Shop is a jewel in the rough. It's home to the Mediocre Music Makers Annabelle and Harley, self-proclaimed rednecks. There is unlikely any other place in the state that comes close to the experience visitors get spending an hour or so with these two characters who are polished hicks.

When visitors arrive at the shop, located just off Route 66 in the old City Meat Market, the oldest building in the sparsely occupied downtown of Erick, they get exactly what the sign outside the building states: WELCOME TO ERICK, OKLAHOMA THE REDNECK CAPITOL OF THE WORLD! YEE-HAW! SEE REDNECKS WORK AND PLAY IN THEIR OWN ENVIRONMENT!

Barefoot and decked out in their redneck tuxedoes, which are red-and-white striped bib overalls, the couple feeds loads of tourists heaping plates of hearty redneck entertainment that is full of lively music, engaging storytelling, and even a bit of raunchy humor. Harley, however, has a keen sense as to how far he can push the envelope with his audience. He's in this for the fun and wants everyone to leave with appetites satisfied, not ruined.

Visitors are warned up front that they're in for some "insanity at its finest." Harley's overgrown beard, long hair, and missing front tooth only add to the boisterous, crass, redneck persona he has so skillfully mastered. Annabelle is animated but has a softer, gentler manner. She is to Harley what Gracie Allen was to George Burns, only redneck style. Since 1999, the sincerity of their act has captured the hearts of international tourists, who have made SandHills Curiosity Shop a featured stop on their trek down Route 66. The couple is featured on foreign television and in-flight videos on airlines, so the tourists are talking about them even before they arrive and long after the leave.

Self-proclaimed rednecks Annabel and Harley (the Mediocre Music Makers) always ready to entertain.

Snacks and cold drinks, even a shot of whiskey if you want, are part of the ambience of the free music show performed by Harley and Annabelle. Harley is an accomplished musician, who played backup with the likes of Charley Pride. If you enjoy your stop, your appreciation can be shown by adding to the tip jars scattered among the valuable antiquities, vintage guitars, signs, and curios that fill this 55-foot by 25-foot shop. Nope, nothing is for sale; it's just for viewing.

Now in their sixties, Harley and Annabelle have been perfecting their act ever since they spontaneously cooked it up in 1999 as a means of entertaining an unexpected bus full of foreign tourists who had interrupted one of their jam sessions. The tour bus was ahead of schedule for a Route 66 attraction in Elk City and needed to kill time so it stopped in Erik. The tourists were attracted to the unusual store front and music coming from inside. Harley and Annabelle's characters also caught the eye of Pixar producers, who used them as inspiration for some of the characters in the animated film *Cars,* set on Route 66.

Harley and Annabelle Russell have a lot more depth and talent than they're willing to publicly reveal. They have definitely found a niche, and it is anything but mediocre.

The shop is open from March through October. Although you're likely to find them in the store rehearsing their music nearly any day, it's best to let them know you're coming. The shop is located at 201 South Sheb Wooley Avenue. For more information call (580) 526-3738.

Geronimooooooo!

Fort Sill

A pile of cobblestones stacked in the shape of a pyramid about 5 feet tall and topped with a regal military eagle marks the gravesite of Geronimo, one of America's most notorious Apache warriors. The grave stands out in the Apache cemetery located on the Fort Sill army base near Lawton, just as Geronimo did among some of the fiercest Indian warriors of the Southwest. Never a chief, Geronimo came to Fort Sill as an older man, who had been a prisoner of war for many years after surrendering in 1886 after his last gruesome raid. Although his ferocity had waned, he continued to be a formidable man who was becoming a living legend. He hated the civilization of white settlers but finally succumbed to the changes and actually embraced the white man's capitalistic ways.

Geronimo's grave sits next to his wife's, ZI-YEH.

While the rest of the Indians held at Fort Sill were eventually allowed to return to their home states, Arizona barred Geronimo's return because of his past bloody deeds, leaving him banished to a life at Fort Sill as a prisoner of war. Geronimo, however, didn't go unnoticed, as his celebrity status began to grow. He had offers to tour with Buffalo Bill's Wild West Show. He appeared at the 1904 Louisiana Purchase Exposition in St. Louis, Missouri, and because of the public's fascination, he was one of the star attractions in President Theodore Roosevelt's 1905 inaugural parade.

Geronimo was even known to have photographs taken of himself that he sold for 50 cents, and he sold autographs for a dollar. During events and train rides when he would get recognized, he also sold the buttons right off his jacket for a quarter as souvenirs only to turn around and attach new buttons at night to be ready for the next day.

Geronimo's popularity has never waned even though he has been dead for nearly a hundred years. The warrior's gravesite and the guard-house holding cell where he spent time are now successful tourist attractions for Fort Sill, drawing visitors to the base daily. In touring the holding cell, you might think that he was kept there because of the war he waged on the white man, but the only time Geronimo actually spent in the holding cell was when he had to sober up from nights of drunk and disorderly conduct.

The great warrior died of pneumonia on February 17, 1909, a week after he spent the night unconscious in the cold and rain. He apparently got drunk in Lawton and on his ride back to Fort Sill fell off his horse.

Nothing Wrong with This Big Head
Granite

A dream to carve the giants of the Great Plains out of granite came to a head in 1979. Bill Willis envisioned carving full-body portraits of three great Oklahomans in a mosaic design that would stand 11 stories high at the foot of the 500-million-year-old mountains that are made out of the rose-colored rock for which the town of Granite is named. The bust

This vision may not have been completed, but Will Rogers's mosiac head is a sight to see.

of humorist Will Rogers is all that materialized from Willis's grand vision to honor Rogers, Olympic gold medalist Jim Thorpe, and Cherokee scholar Sequoyah.

"I just couldn't get enough money to do it," said Willis, who in 1979 estimated the project would cost $3 million to complete.

"I've put $50,000 in just Will Rogers's head," he said.

The bust sits off Highway 9 at the granite quarry owned by Willis. Sightseers visit the site nearly every day, he said.

The plan, Willis said, was to have a free tourist attraction that would boost the state's economy. He had hoped to profit in the long-term with higher land values on other property he owned in town.

Schooled to be an architect, Willis brought a touch of design to the family's Granite Products business. He said he saw a canvas for skin in the pink stone and began developing a technique of soft shading that has become the company's trademark. Concerned about the artistic look of the mosaic project, Willis used with permission an artist's painting to ensure the sculpture looked like the subject. Nearly three decades later, Willis still gets compliments about the Will Roger mosaic.

Willis gives tours of his facility, which is located next-door to the tribute to Will Rogers. His facility carves granite products, mostly gravestones. Other products include countertops, historical markers, and portraits. Willis said granite is everywhere in the town; it's in the buildings, the schools, and even the curbs.

The huge granite bust of Will Rogers is located on 900 Quarry Drive. Tours of the Willis granite facility are available by appointment only by calling (580) 535-2184.

YOU ARE AN OKIE IF . . .

You can properly pronounce all of the following town names: Ouachita, Pushmataha, Sapulpa, Miami, Okemah, Tishomingo, Boise City, Wapanucka, and Chickasha.

You don't think it's odd to see chicken-fried steak on the menu.

You know exactly what calf fries are and you eat them anyway.

A BMW is nothing compared to a Ford four-wheel drive.

You put peppered cream gravy on everything.

You understand the meaning of "dry county," "liquor-by-the-drink," "once saved, always saved," and Vacation Bible School.

You understand the difference between 3.2 and 6.0 beer and know what a beer run to the other state is.

Your place at the lake has wheels.

You know the value of a parking space is judged by the amount of the shade.

You live in a town with a name like Hooker, Beaver, Pink, or Bowlegs.

It's Not Just Another Dance Floor

Hobart

Kiowa County Commissioner Leiland Osmond floored everyone in Hobart a decade ago when he decided to tile a portion of the Kiowa County Courthouse lawn so dances and other activities could be held there. The tiles, however, aren't just any tiles. The hand-painted tiles depict the history of Kiowa County, drawn in a Norman Rockwell sort of style. It is touted as one of the largest mosaics in the country.

The largest mosaic in the nation is of Kiowa County on a concrete slab in the courtyard of the Kiowa County Courthouse.

"It's just something I dreamt up one night," said Osmond.

The sheriff kept talking about the courtyard and the need for a hard surface so dances and other activities could be performed during festivals. Already concerned that the county was losing a lot of its historical sites, Osmond saw the courtyard as an opportunity to preserve history.

"One thing led to another, and I woke up one morning and said: 'I've got it! A map. I'll put a historic map of Kiowa County on a slab,'" Osmond said, and the Kiowa County Mosaic Tile Project was born.

Laying the 56-foot by 53-foot concrete slab was easy. The hard work, Osmond said, was deciding what to use to cover the slab, who to hire to draw the map, and how to pay for it. A challenge was all Osmond needed to inspire him to make his dream come true. It was decided that the flooring would be tile, a Texas artist would draw the map, and the bulk of the hundred-thousand-dollar price tag would come from the state with the rest borne by the county and private funds. Tile by tile, residents watched a colorful map depicting Kiowa County's historical sites, cemeteries, and one-room schools emerge on the gray concrete slab. Tiles commemorating the town's veterans were also included in the design. Today visitors come to Hobart to view the mosaic slab and to photograph it. The mosaic sits next to the gazebo on the courthouse square located at 316 South Main Street. For more information call (580) 726-2553.

Getting Stalked

Hydro

Cornfields abound in western Oklahoma, but the Liebscher's P_Bar Farms on Route 66 in Hydro stands out among all others—or one may say it is outstanding in its field, its field of corn. What makes Loren and Kim Liebscher's eight-acre cornfield unique is that this corn is not planted to become maize, but to become a maze. What sprouts into sight even before you reach the entrance is the big barn roof with The MAZE painted on top.

The centennial corn maze celebrating Oklahoma's one-hundredth birthday at P_Bar Farms.

Several years ago, the Liebschers took the dying hundred-year-old family farm and, with the help of a GPS and a push lawnmower, combined agriculture and entertainment, creating an extraordinary agritainment venue. Every year the Liebschers create a different theme for their popular maze. Their first maze was "Get Lost on Route 66" and the 2007 maze honored Oklahoma's centennial. Between the first week of September and the third week of November, P_Bar Farms is open to visitors who wish to lose themselves in the three hundred thousand corn stalks that create the corn labyrinth. Composed of two separate sections, the entire maze takes about an hour to get through—thirty minutes if you choose to indulge in only one side of corn. Since the maze stands 7 feet high, Corn Cops are available to help visitors find the exit and to ensure that no visitor is left alone to be stalked.

The Halloween season has the Liebschers again differing from other corn farmers by the way they shuck the idea that corn is grown for creaming but instead is grown for screaming. During the last two weeks of October, the maze becomes the Haunted Maze at night. Visitors make their way through the darkened maze with nothing but glow sticks to light their way, as dozens of spooks and goblins pop out of the corn to give them an unforgettable scare. There is a less frightening haunted barn for the youngsters.

P_Bar Farms' agritainment also includes a twelve-acre pumpkin patch, a tractor-pulled train ride, a petting zoo, and a concession area with plenty of seating. It's guaranteed that if you trek to Hydro, you'll find yourself up to your ears in an A-MAZE-ING experience. The farm is located on Route 66 between Hydro and Weatherford. If traveling Interstate 40 take exit 84 westbound or exit 88 eastbound and follow Route 66 north. For more information call (580) 772-4401 or visit www .pbarfarms.com.

GREAT PLAINS COUNTRY

This Land is HER Land
Lawton

In a time when women were oppressed by society's predetermined role for them, Mattie Beal dared to break away and let chance dictate her future. At age twenty-two, this Kansan threw her name into the 1901 land lottery when the federal government opened up a portion of southeast Oklahoma near Fort Sill for settlement despite her mother's fear that such an adventure was much too danger-ous for a young single woman.

The historic Mattie Beal home.

To her mother's surprise and worry, Beal's name was the second drawn from the lottery box by one of ten blindfolded boys, putting her in a great position to choose 160 acres of land outside of Lawton. But James Wood, who won the first drawing, planned to thwart any chance of Beal getting a piece of prime property. Wood veered from the traditional manner of claiming land in the shape of a square and instead mapped out his 160 acres in the shape of an *L* hogging the southern border of Lawton. Woods believed that since his staked-out property abutted the town boundary that settlers would most likely want to purchase his land for homesteads. Wood's cunning move, which forced Beal to file her claim farther from town, backfired. Beal still had Lady Luck looking over her. Beal's choice on higher ground proved to be more valuable because every time it rained, it was Wood's property in the lower Squaw Creek Bottom that flooded, not hers.

Beal's prime land and her kindness and gregarious personality gained her instant fame along with a barrage of suitors. Beal quickly made her property affordable to settlers who couldn't afford land elsewhere. She also donated land for a church, a school, and two parks, and promoted culture in the city.

Of all the suitors seeking to marry Beal, it was Charles Payne, owner of a local lumber company, who won her hand. The two built a fourteen-room Italian and Greek Revival–style mansion in 1909 on the corner of Fifth and Summit Streets, where the couple reared three daughters. Beal continued to promote culture in the city, becoming the belle of early Lawton society. She also continued, along with her husband, to help those less fortunate, especially during the Great Depression. The Mattie Beal Mansion was the first landmark in Lawton to be placed on the National Register of Historic Places. The mansion can be toured by appointment. For more information or to make an appointment, call (580) 678-5156 or visit www.lawtonheritage.org.

This Park Has Gone To the Dogs

Lawton

Lawton was home to hundreds of prairie dogs long before the town was divvied up to settlers during a land lottery in 1901 and even before the establishment of Fort Sill in 1869. The prairie dogs are still there, despite attempts to rid them from the area.

They can be easily spotted in one of the city's main public gathering spots, Elmer Thomas Park.

Prairie dogs have their own town in Elmer Thomas Park.

Many people find the prairie dogs frolicking around in town and in rural pastures quite harmless. Others, mainly ranchers, find them a hazard because they create numerous holes in the ground that can cripple livestock. The ranchers want them gone at any cost. It's not uncommon for ranchers to allow hunters onto their private property to shoot the prairie dogs. After all, prairie dogs are rodents, ranchers argue. It may be hard for the average person to imagine the cute little prairie dog in the same category as rats and mice, but technically they are. Actually, they're cousins to the squirrel. They multiply quickly and there are no boundaries to the size of their underground town of tunnels.

The cute little critters, however, are quite entertaining to watch as they pop out of their holes, hands held high as though to show you they mean no harm. They play and scurry around after food to nibble on as they sit on their haunches looking at you looking at them before darting back into their burrows. The show can easily fill time on a lazy day in the park.

In the late 1990s Lawton officials considered eradicating the thousands of dogs that had invaded Elmer Thomas Park but realized their plan was too politically hot to handle. Instead, the officials decided to capitalize on the dogs rather than euthanize them. It now uses the prairie dog town in the park as a hook for tourists. While the city does periodically thin the population through a relocation program, it claims to have the largest and friendliest prairie dog town. Elmer Thomas Park is located at Third Street and Ferris Avenue. For more information on the dogs, contact the Lawton Chamber of Commerce at (580) 355-3541.

Beauty Is in the Eye of the Beholder

Lawton

When Claude and Lynda Burrell sit in their front yard at their strategically placed patio table, people stop and some even want to shop. The problem is that the trinkets, antiques, and odds and ends adorning the lawn around Claude and Lynda are not for sale. They are merely yard enhancers, displayed for others to interpret.

"I call their yard a league of its own, because they're in a league of their own," said neighbor, Pearl Newton as she makes a gesture with her hand like a game-show model directing your attention to the objects.

Claude and Lynda Burrell stand on their front porch behind yard decorations that are erected all year long.

"They have so much stuff that after awhile, you sit back and say, 'Hey, maybe that doesn't look that bad,'" she said before releasing a hardy laugh.

The Burrells have been adding, rearranging, and just sitting and admiring the medley of objects for the past five years in front of their two-story home, which was built in 1905. Their home is located in the 200 block of Summit Avenue. The lot is part of the original 160-acre allotment of Lawton's Mattie Beal, whose historic mansion is located just a few blocks away. Historical or hysterical, it's hard to say which home gets the most visitors.

"People in town think we're crazy. I can't tell you how many times someone has offered me money for something thinking we're having a yard sale. Like that stove over there," said Claude pointing to a slender, 2-foot-tall, single-burner, antique, cast-iron stove his wife carted from California.

The stuff ranges from a row of artificial Christmas trees along a fence separating the front and back yards to a mermaid statue that Lynda found headless. She mended it with cement and painted it gold. There's a yard jockey, rocks and driftwood with trinkets glued on them, a hodge-podge of ceramic statues, and even a modern cloth-covered chair shaped like a high-heeled shoe, but it's broken so it leans against a porch post. Lynda finds most of the stuff discarded and broken in the street or in someone's garbage can. While mending the things she finds, she nearly always adds something of her own, creating new and original yard art.

The Burrells can spot newcomers because they drive by real slowly, and if one of the Burrells is outside, the newcomers will stop to talk. There is no doubt Lynda has an eye for junk. Everyone else's trash is her treasure.

The couple enjoys visiting with those who stop by, so don't be shy.

This Town Is All Washed Up
Lugert

Lugert still draws sightseers even though it isn't really a town anymore. The town still sits on its original site, which is now at the bottom of Lake Altus-Lugert. Remains of the town emerge occasionally during dry spells when the water level recedes and when water is siphoned from the lake once a year for irrigation purposes. During those times, hikers willing to tackle patches of cockleburs can explore the old town site finding slabs, crumbled foundations, wells, and the most distinguishable structure, the cellar of the old Lugert School.

There is something to be said of this small town that refuses to be forgotten. It was all but destroyed by a tornado in 1912 , after which part of the town was rebuilt with stone from the area. It was the only small town of its time that no longer had wooden structures. Like many other towns across the state, Lugert fell victim to the Dust Bowl and its already small population dwindled. It continued to survive up until the late1940s when construction of the dam for the lake was complete and the town was submerged.

Once the lake was full, the town's buildings could be seen just below the surface of the water, giving the state its own city of Atlantis. In the 1980s many of the buildings were partially knocked down due to the hazards they posed for boaters. During the drought of 1998, water levels were so low that treasure hunters flocked to the area after news that old silverware and coins were being found along the shore.

Frank Lugert founded the town in 1901. Not only did Lugert, a Czech immigrant, plat the area, open the first general store, and establish a post office, but he also issued his own stamped coin currency that locals could use in his establishments. The town site, which sat in the valley near the foot of the Wichita Mountains, had plenty of farmland, freshwater, and a railroad—all the necessities for a community to thrive. The mountainous area drew ranchers, outlaws, and miners digging for copper or secretly searching for Spanish gold that allegedly was buried in the area, according to legend.

One of the many stories recounted about the town's heyday is about how friendly the Lugerts were with the outlaws who would hide in the mountains and replenish their supplies at Lugert General Store. Apparently, the outlaws would show up in the middle of the night or in the predawn hours, and Mrs. Lugert would feed them for free. If they couldn't pay for supplies, well, they were free too. It's unclear whether it was fear that motivated the Lugerts' generosity or the realization that being kind to the outlaws was likely a wise move for both their overall wealth and health. Unlike others in the area, the Lugerts were never robbed. According to Lugert's granddaughter, a couple of armed men did come to the store demanding liquor once, but all Lugert had was

A city exposed.

Hostetter's Bitters, a patent medicine that was 70 percent alcohol. It worked and the hooligans left without incident.

Lugert is located along the eastern dike of the lake just north of the dam off Highway 44. Hikers need to be watchful of the uncovered wells in the area. For more information contact Quartz Mountain State Park at (580) 563-2238.

Half the Battle is the Marketing
Medicine Park

The national fascination with the Canadian-born Dionne quintuplets during the Great Depression was not limited to Medicine Park, Oklahoma, which used the quintuplets to boost cabin rentals at the state's first tourism resort town. The small town is off Highway 49 nestled along the banks of Medicine Creek, which flows into Lake Lawtonka.

The birth of the first quintuplets in North American brought instant fame to the dark-haired baby girls and to Dr. Allan Roy Dafoe, who delivered the historic fivesome in 1934 and took over their guardianship. For the next decade, the girls were used in a whirlwind of advertising endorsements and host of commercial products selling themselves—paper dolls, baby dolls, calendars, and in Medicine Park, five single-room, cobblestone cabins all in a row, each bearing a Dionne quin name. Still there and still occasionally rented out are cabins named Yvonne, Annette, Marie, Emilie, and Cecile.

The owner of the cabins, Dora Kramer, said back in the early days of Medicine Park all of the cabins and buildings in town had names. When these five cabins were built in 1940s, the then owner decided the names of the Dionne quins would be perfect names for the cabins. It was just the gimmick needed for an edge in the rental competition of the popular resort town.

By the 1960s, when Kramer and her husband, Les, purchased the cabins, the Dionne quintuplets were all but forgotten with the dawning of the age of Aquarius. Dora, however, was a devoted fan of the quins, owning many of the dolls and Dionne paraphernalia. She would really get upset with soldiers from nearby Fort Sill who came to town wanting to rent one of those cabins, thinking it came with a prostitute bearing the cabin's name.

Although the Kramers keep the cabins freshly painted with the girls' names, they may have a bit of a promotion problem due to Dora's insistence on referring to the girls as the famous "quads." When asked if she means "quins" because there are five of them, she just smiles and says with confidence: "Quads, quins, whatever; we've always called them the quads down here."

For lodging information call (580) 529-2974.

Dora Kramer stands in front of one of the five cabins named after the Canadian-born Dionne quintuplets.

Seismic Burgers
Meers

There aren't many burger joints that can draw crowds to the middle of nowhere like the Meers Store and Restaurant can. Customers will drive hundreds of miles to wait in line for the Meers Burger, a half-pounder of Texas Longhorn beef snuggled in a 7-inch bun and served on a pie tin.

The restaurant and store, located in a nearly ninety-year-old building, sits on Highway 115 just north of the Wichita Mountains Wildlife Refuge. Joe and Margie Maranto, owners since 1983, attribute the restaurant's success to using the beef from their range-fed Longhorn herd. The 97 percent lean beef is ground daily at the store.

Meers waitress Ashley Conte displays the restaurant's famous Longhorn burger.

"It's the restaurant's reputation that's the draw. How else do you get people way out here? We're out in the middle of nowhere, and I guess that's a good thing that we're the only thing in nowhere because people come here for a reason," Maranto said.

It's hard to debunk Maranto's claims. There is no doubt that the restaurant is a destination point, not just a happenstance drive-by. The restaurant is all that remains of the town of Meers formed in 1901 by a hoax that gold could be found in the Wichitas. Gold fever was bad here and pretty much nobody survived. Only a few ranchers remain. Nearby to the south of Meers is the refuge, but to the north there is no town for tens of miles. So there is no real reason for anyone to just be driving by.

Come 11:30 a.m. nearly every day, customers start showing up. A line is formed by noon and into the afternoon. The majority of the customers are seeking the featured item—a Meers burger served cowboy style with mustard, tomato, red onion, and leaf lettuce, "not the cheap iceberg lettuce," Maranto said. Cheese is extra.

"Occasionally someone will ask for mayo and I tell them that we call that the sissy burger. If someone asks for ketchup, that's a Yankee burger; you see, we think ketchup should stay on the fries," he said.

Due to the popularity of high-protein diets, the restaurant also offers what it calls the Grubsteak, a 4-, 8-, or whopping 16-ounce patty served either with grilled onions, cheese, bacon, or jalapenos, or all four. It's whatever the customer wants minus the bun. The burgers aren't the only menu items. Hotdogs, steaks, and barbecue fixings are also available. The topper to any meal is the homemade dessert, which consists of pies, cobblers, and ice cream made with real butter cream.

Maranto will tell you that the customers come in hungry and leave full—the perfect recipe for success. There is definitely a gold mine in Meers, and that's no hoax. The restaurant is open every day except Tuesday. Call (580) 429-8051 for hours.

There's a Whole Lot of Shaking Going On Here

Meers

California isn't the only place that quakes. Oklahoma has been known to rumble now and then.

The Meers fault stretches across Oklahoma. It is the only surface-breaking rupture east of the Rocky Mountains and the first in ten thousand years to have documented movement in this region.

In 1985 the Oklahoma Geological Survey Observatory established one of the most sensitive international seismograph stations in the country here, called the Meers Observatory. The Meers Store and Restaurant houses a seismograph that is connected by cable to a seismometer in a mine shaft about 2,000 feet northwest of the restaurant. Restaurant owners Joe and Margie Maranto and their staff voluntarily monitor the equipment.

The Meers Observatory has registered Russian nuclear tests, a natural gas explosion in Brenham, Texas, and an earthquake on an island in the Indian Ocean—more than ten thousand miles away. It took twenty minutes for the quake vibrations to cut through the earth to Meers.

There was an earthquake in Oklahoma in 1987 and Kingfisher County registered the quake at a magnitude of 3.7. Another quake hit in 1990 about 55 miles from Meers in Gavin County. In 1997 another tremor with a magnitude of 2.0 was recorded 17 miles from Meers but close enough to break the pin on the seismograph. The state has registered 695 earthquakes in sixty-four of its seventy-seven counties from 1977 through 1990.

The seismograph can be viewed in the restaurant, which is located on Highway 115 about 1.5 miles north of the Wichita Mountains Wildlife Refuge. The restaurant is open every day except Tuesday. For more information call (580) 429-8051.

Fifteen Minutes of Fame

Sayre

The sleepy town of Sayre has had its share of the limelight over the decades. The brightest light may have shone on the landmark Beckham County Courthouse that towers over the east end of Main Street. The neoclassical, Renaissance–revival style courthouse was featured in the 1940 film, *The Grapes of Wrath,* based on John Steinbeck's classic American novel of the same title. The courthouse had less than a minute of time on the big screen, but it was enough to give the city a claim to fame.

The town was also home to the world's largest known source of helium, producing over 8 billion cubic feet of gas from 1973 to 1993 out of the Panhandle-Hugoton field.

It's unclear whether the abundance of helium in the area had any influence on balloonist Maxie Anderson, a Sayre native. In 1978 he, along with two other men, was the first to cross the Atlantic Ocean in a balloon, the *Double Eagle II.*

Beckham County Courthouse was featured in the film The Grapes of Wrath.

BECKHAM COUNTY COURTHOUSE

Also in the area is the site of a historic twenty-three-thousand-year-old buffalo kill, estimated to have the remains of eight hundred bison, according the to Oklahoma Archaeological Survey. Between 300 B.C. and A.D. 300, bison were killed when herders chased them over sandstone cliffs. The site is located on the Flying W, a private working ranch. For directions and more information call (888) 928-8864.

These Rattles Aren't for Babies
Waurika

People from across the region come to the south central Oklahoma town of Waurika each spring to participate in the oldest rattler roundup in the country—the "Fangtastic" Rattlesnake Hunt. Armed with canvas bags and 20-inch-long metal tongs, hordes of fearless fang finders search the outskirts of Waurika for lethal rattlesnakes hidden in the nearby hilly and rocky landscape.

This longstanding tradition was initially started nearly fifty years ago as a way to reduce the population of slithering reptiles that wreaked havoc on ranchers' livestock by crippling horses, cattle, and sheep. It didn't take long, however, for hunt organizers to realize the efforts were futile. These rattling serpents weren't going away. Nor should they have to, animal rights activists argue.

Effective or not, controversial or not, Waurika residents were not about to give up a tradition that has evolved into a successful fundraising event for the Volunteer Fire Department. The three-day hunt draws thousands of people into the area in early April. Fireman Johnny Berry said the growing market for rattlesnake venom, meat, and pelts makes it all more worthwhile.

Most of the snake hunters enter the roundup for bragging rights, Berry said. It's a battle to see who can find the largest serpent or the rattler that festival officials have marked with a pink stripe and released into the hunting area. There are two secrets to capturing the reptiles—first, you have to know where to find them, and second, you have to know how to roust them without getting fanged, he said.

The lively event is not for anyone squeamish about snakes, because there are snakes everywhere. Snake handlers offer demonstrations of the rattler's natural abilities. You can be photographed with a snake if you don't mind a venomous viper draped over your shoulders. The real test, however, lies in the ability to stomach the "Butcher Shoppe." It is downright gruesome. Surprisingly, the gruesome demonstration doesn't stop crowds of festival goers from gathering to watch butchers, splattered with blood and guts, behead and then skin snakes. The pelts are placed in one pile, the meat in another, and both are for sale.

Hayden Latta operates the butcher shop where the rattlesnakes are skinned.

Despite the fear and gore factor, the festival does have a carnival atmosphere, featuring a host of vendors selling a host of goods including snakeskin items. Of course, the featured food is deep-fried rattlesnake meat, which kind of tastes like chicken. But then, again doesn't nearly everything taste like chicken?

For more information about the festival, call (580) 228-2553 or visit www.rattlesnakehunt.com.

SNAKE, RATTLE, AND ROLL

Each spring rattlesnake hunts, roundups, and festivals are held throughout the state. While Waurika's hunt is one of the oldest in the state, other communities like Apache, Mangum, Okeene, and Waynoka also hold events that have become traditions and boost their local economies.

Some of the festivals are:

Apache Rattlesnake Festival held in mid–April. For information call (580) 588-3361.

Mangum Rattlesnake Derby held in late April. For information call (580) 782-2434.

Okeene Annual Rattlesnake Hunt held in April. For information call (580) 822-3101.

Waynoka Snake Hunt held in late April. For information call (580) 824-1471.

RED CARPET COUNTRY

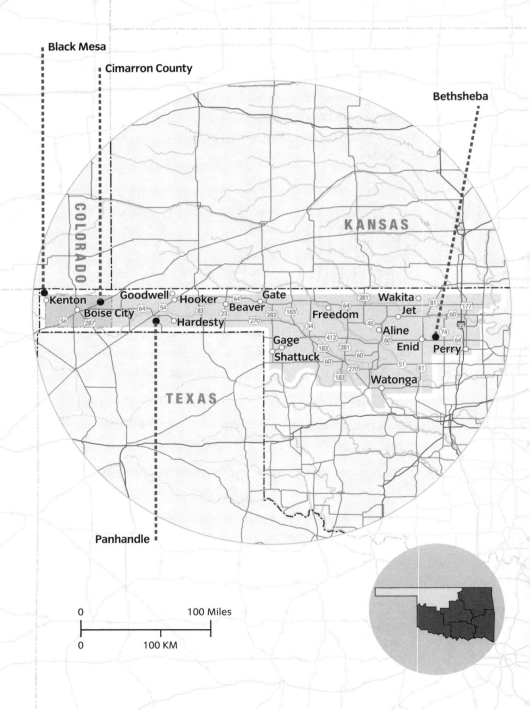

Black Mesa

Cimarron County

Bethsheba

COLORADO

KANSAS

Kenton Goodwell Hooker Gate Wakita
Boise City 54 Beaver Jet
56 287 23 283 183 Freedom 177
Hardesty 270 Aline 81 60
Gage 412 Enid 74 Perry
Shattuck 281 60 64
TEXAS 60 51 81
270
183 Watonga

Panhandle

0   100 Miles

0   100 KM

RED CARPET COUNTRY

If you've ever wanted to walk down the red carpet, you don't need to go to Hollywood. You can just go to the Oklahoma Panhandle area, otherwise known as Red Carpet Country, named for the dark red dirt created by an enormous prehistoric sea that once covered the region. Other signs of prehistoric activity abound in Red Carpet Country. The highest point in Oklahoma, Black Mesa, boasts of not only volcanic rock formations, but also dinosaur tracks and pits, out of which more than eighteen tons of fossilized dinosaur bones have been excavated. The region also has the salt of the earth, literally, in the Great Salt Plains, an actual sea of salt that is the only place in the world people can dig for hourglass selenite crystals.

Red Carpet Country is also home to other fascinating geological wonders. The Alabaster Caverns, the world's largest gypsum-lined caverns located close to Freedom, Oklahoma, intrigue their visitors with how an underground sea affected the land 200 million years ago. The awesome effects of running water can also be seen in the caverns of Roman Nose Park, close to Watonga.

Water was not the only thing to run into the Oklahoma Panhandle and leave a mark. In the late 1800s, an area of the Panhandle was coined "No Man's Land" because it was sparsely populated, unorganized, and unprotected. Robbers' Roost, situated in Black Mesa State Park, was a hideout for outlaw gangs, who would prey upon unsuspecting souls in the area and on wagon trains traveling the Santa Fe Trail.

Whatever your interest is, whether it is to view the phenomenal geographical wonders or to wonder at the human phenomenon in the area, run through Oklahoma's Red Carpet Country and leave your mark. As always, the red carpet will be laid out for you.

Home Turf
Aline

Marshall and Sadie McCully had a knack for weeding through the rough times, living in a two-room "soddy," which happens to now be the only sod home built by a homesteader that still exists in the state. Their soddy is located just outside of Aline inside the Sod House Museum. Yep, a sense of humor and bit of grit were essential elements that luckily both McCullys possessed during the late 1800s when the untamed land of Oklahoma Territory was opened up to settlers.

Marshall, a Missourian, made claim to the land first and then to Sadie, a schoolteacher from the nearby town of Enid. This educated woman willingly packed a couple of trunks, purchased a walnut dresser and an upright organ, and started her married life in a home made from Buffalo grass.

Marshall scraped off a one-half-acre site of sod and cut it into blocks that he used to build the house. He used the Alkali clay that lined a nearby creek bed as plaster to cover the walls and keep insects out. Flour sacks were hung horizontally like hammocks across the ceiling to capture loose dirt, debris, and intruding snakes. The thick earthen walls kept the home cool in the summer and was easy to heat in the winter with virtually no fear of structural fires that were so common with the wood-frame homes.

Together the couple lived a hard yet happy life with organ music as the primary means of entertainment. Those days came to a halt in 1896 after a sickly Sadie gave birth to their daughter, Letha, and was unable to nurse the baby. Financially broke and with only one cow that was dry, the couple agreed to trade Sadie's treasured organ for a healthy milk cow, which Sadie decided to call "Old Organ." Letha grew to be a healthy young girl. Sadie's health, however, grew worse, and she died six years later. She is buried in the Aline Star Cemetery.

The only remaining sod house in the state.

Marshall remarried Pearle, a city girl from Wichita, Kansas, who worked as a milliner. Life on a farm and living in a sod house was trying and downright amusing. Pearle never lived down the time she tried to bury some dough. Embarrassed by her lack of culinary skills when her bread dough failed to rise, she and Letha buried it in the orchard to hide the mistake. A few hours later after the sun had warmed the ground, Marshall strolled by and noticed this newly formed huge mound. He pierced it with a shovel to find gooey dough ready for the oven.

Nobody knows why the McCully sod house endured while others succumbed to the extreme weather elements. In 1910 Marshall McCully built a two-story frame house next to the sod house, which was used as a place for storing produce and meat, until Marshall died in 1963. That same year, the Oklahoma Historical Society purchased the sod house to further preserve it and the colorful life of living in a soddy.

Admission to the Sod House Museum is free. It is closed Monday and state holidays. For more information call (405) 463-2441.

This is One B.S. Story
Beaver

Taking a pile of crap from your competitors is an annual event in Beaver at the World Cow Chip Throwing Championship. Every April people from around the region, and even from out-of-state, converge on this small community to bare-handedly pitch poop. Some may chuckle to think that what cows discard could be the key to creating a town's uniqueness. But, when this typical ranching town went looking to reinvent itself, it went no farther than its pastures, capitalizing on what it had plenty of— piles of bovine manure, more fondly called "chips."

The prized disc used in Beaver's annual World Cup Cow Chip Throwing Championship.

These Beaverites are no different than the residents before them, who turned the sun-dried droppings into a commodity. Settlers collected the chips by the wagonloads to fuel the flames in stoves, fireplaces, and even campfires, because of the odorless, sootless, intense heat it produced. This time around, the chips are heating up the competition for those folks who believe they can fling the disc-shaped turd the farthest. The B.S. Enterprise Committee combs pastures for the brown gold looking for just the right shape and weight to use for the competition.

The contestants, who must be no younger than sixteen years old, select two chips from those gathered by the B.S. committee. Each is at least 6 inches in diameter. Any alteration of those chips could cost competitors a 25-foot penalty.

World record throws were set at the Beaver event in 2001 by Robby Deevers of Liberal, Kansas, who threw his chip 185 feet, 5 inches, and Dana Martin of Goodwell, Oklahoma, who threw hers 146 feet, 6 inches.

This sanctioned chip-tossing event was started in 1970 by a group of Beaver businessmen seeking to gas up the annual Cimarron Territory Celebration that began in 1937 to honor the pioneers who in 1887 unsuccessfully tried to get Congress to designate the Panhandle a separate U.S. territory called Cimarron. The businessmen's quest to add the tossing of aged, sun-dried buffalo and cow chips to the annual celebration was quite easy and a tremendous success. The throwing event is held on the last day of the seven-day Cimarron Territory Celebration that usually runs the second week of April.

"That first fling put Beaver back on the map, and that's no B.S.," said Kirk Fisher, one of the founding members of the event.

For more information about the event, contact the Beaver County Chamber of Commerce at (580) 625-4726.

Here One Minute, Gone the Next
Beaver

Unexplainable activity lurking in and around a town often makes town officials want to go stick their heads in the sand. Not such a good idea in Beaver, where it's rumored that somewhere hidden in the sand dunes of Beaver State Park is a little known enigma purported to be a gateway into another world.

Town and state officials say they know nothing about this supposed gateway that abducts people from the park. They seem puzzled at the very notion such a thing could exist. Members of the paranormal community, however, claim to be all too familiar with the Shamen's Portal, or so they think they are. They claim there have been small expeditions secretly holding covert digs at the dunes since 1993. The 360 acres of sand hills do appear to come out of nowhere in the Panhandle's prairie,

The Bermuda Triangle of Oklahoma.

just outside this quaint town. The sand hills are a popular spot for dune-buggy activities.

"Nobody has turned up missing as far as I know," said City Manager Don Jenkins. "Are they saying we have some type of Bermuda Triangle deal?"

According to the chatter among paranormalists on Internet sites and blogs, yes, people have vanished in plain sight. Poof! Gone. They claim that the disappearances date back to Francisco Vásquez de Coronado during his expedition to find the fabled Seven Cities of Cibola. Part of his travels took him through the Panhandle near Beaver and the sand dunes.

The legend is that three of Coronado's soldiers disappeared in a blinding flash of green light. A friar on the expedition documented the event in his journal, calling it the work "of El Diablo." It's alleged that a member of the expedition also recorded it but was later ordered by Coronado to remove any reference of it from his journal, creating one of the biggest cover-ups ever. Apparently, some paranormalists believe people continued to vanish in a green light up until 1987. There are reports that even famed Texan Jim Bowie tried to track down the reported paranormal activity during the 1800s.

On one Internet thread about the sand dunes, a person claims he participated in a secret expedition to the area after hearing that the military supposedly uncovered some sort of cylinder there in 1995. Apparently the secret expedition found samplings of ionized soil cores and electromagnetic interference that registered off the scale. This alleged discovery now has some pondering whether the portal was actually a buried space vehicle.

Kirk Fisher, a former town official, is skeptical of the wild claims. But, if he were forced to choose, he said he likely would lean toward space aliens.

"That is probably the reason none of us know anything about this. The aliens sucked that memory right out of our brains," he said wiggling his fingers on either side of his temples.

RED CARPET COUNTRY

"I can tell you what I do believe. Somebody has been watching too many episodes of *X-Files*," he said with a smile.

Beaver State Park allows motorcycles, dune buggies, ATVs, and 4x4s on the sand dunes. For more information call (580) 625-3373.

Oklahoma's Own Sappho
Bethsheba

It's hard to know if the settlement of Bethsheba really existed or if it was just a feminine figment of someone's imagination. Maybe it was a tale concocted and passed down through generations to discourage women from considering a life free of a male influence and domination. While there is no documentation that verifies it existed briefly in 1893 somewhere in Garfield County between Enid and Perry, there are a few unattributed accounts with interesting facts about the town at the Cherokee Strip Museum in Perry and a few theories floating around.

It is reported that the all-female commune barred all males—humans and animals alike. There were absolutely no men, no stallions, no boars, no bulls, no roosters, or even tomcats allowed. The settlement was supposedly formed by a group of disgruntled women that were anti-men. Because reporters at the time were male, those who attempted to write about Bethsheba were forced to do it from afar using binoculars and assumptions. Of course, in those days when land runs drew single women willing to stake land without a husband, and settlement came and went as often as the winds shifted, who would know whether Bethsheba was fact or fiction?

One report claims the town had thirty-three women, but by the end of the first week, a dozen females deserted. At its height of existence, the town reportedly had a mayor, police chief, and a town board. A Kansas reporter wrote that one of the founders also was exiled after she was found with a razor. Apparently masculine implements "were subversive to the vital anti-male principles of the community," the reporter said. This male reporter, who claimed to have gained access into Bethsheba, said he recognized the mayor as a Kansas woman bitter from being conned into marriage by a married man. The reporter ended his article as follows:

Let us waive the throes of blighted affection, and the pangs of a heart without an affinity, which must have driven them to this extremity. Let us be practical. These women have renounced the opposite sex; they have banished it from their heart-stones. But hold! Is not the primal object of every community perpetuity? Can this retreat of women have a continued existence, and a value in the world, under this one-sided single sex system? In a word, can there be a cackle without a crow? We wot [know] not.

Apparently the managing editor didn't buy the reporter's rhetoric. Unsatisfied, he ordered the writer to return to Bethsheba for names that validated his claims. One account states he returned to find abandoned equipment and empty dwellings. Another states he returned to find nothing, no tents, wagons, or even livestock. The town had just disappeared. Some say the women vanished in the middle of the night and were either ambushed by a pack of men or lonely for the security of men. I'd like to think that if there was a Bethsheba its demise came because the women realized that strength and independence came from within and not necessarily at the price of isolation.

To read more about the town, visit the Cherokee Strip Museum in Perry. Call 580-336-2406 for museum hours.

Rocky Mountain High—Okie Style

Black Mesa

Oklahoma's black jewel can be found in the western tip of the panhandle —it's Black Mesa State Park. Standing 4,973 feet above sea level, the mesa is the highest point in Oklahoma. A challenging 4-mile hike to the top takes you to a granite monument marking the highest point in the state.

The mesa is part of the foothills of the Rocky Mountains and provides a spectacular landscape of cactus, lava, and dwarfed vegetation. It extends about 50 miles, with most of it in Colorado. The Black Mesa got its name from the thick layer of black rock formed from lava that covered the region tens of millions years ago. The region dates back to the Jurassic and Triassic periods and contains the fossil remains of dinosaurs.

This 349-acre park is a haven for bird-watchers and ornithologists. In this area birds from both the east and west can be spotted. The park is also popular with highpointer clubs and stargazers. The Okie-Tax Star party is held here every October because the skies in the area are the clearest and darkest.

For information on camping and fishing in the park, contact the Black Mesa State Park manager at (580) 426-2222.

Truman Tucker posing at the highest point monument.

Sometimes Close Is Good Enough

Black Mesa

In a pasture not far from Black Mesa State Park, three people can form a circle by holding hands and each be standing in a different state. The site is in the northwest corner of Oklahoma's Panhandle where Oklahoma's, Colorado's, and New Mexico's borders meet. Since 1900, a three-state marker has stood on that very intersection where the states touch.

Three-state marker showing Oklahoma, Colorado and New Mexico borders.

The marker is supposedly located where the thirty-seventh parallel north latitude intersects 103 degrees west longitude. Apparently it wasn't that easy finding that exact spot. It took surveyors four attempts, and they really never got it exact. The first try was in 1857, the second in 1859, and the third in 1881, but all were incorrect. Then in 1900, reportedly Levi Preston surveyed and determined the fourth site, which was officially accepted and a monument marker was erected. It is speculated that the earlier errors were caused by surveyors favoring a specific territory, the lack of accurate equipment, or the discrepancies over where one territory began and the other ended. Eventually, Congress got involved to determine the exact location.

Time and the advancement of technology, however, have proven Preston's survey also to be slightly off the mark, although very close. But since the marker locating the "official boundary" has gone untouched for one-hundred years, should we care if it isn't in the exact location? If you ask any of the Okies that know about the marker, they don't.

The original marker was made of sandstone, and in 1908 that marker was replaced with the current granite marker. For directions to the three-state marker, contact Black Mesa State Park at (580) 426-2222.

Oklahoma CURIOSITIES

Hole Lot of Fun
Boise City

Out on the plains of the Oklahoma Panhandle, there are only a few things around to see: the horizon, the blue sky, lots of grass, and miles of fencing. So, when Boise City residents went looking for a special contest to invigorate its long-standing Santa Fe Trail Daze celebration, they turned to something familiar to everyone—posthole digging. In 1974 the first World Champion Posthole Digging contest was held.

"Any rancher worth his salt has dug a lot of postholes," said Jay Carson, a former chairman of the event.

Many towns in Oklahoma hold imaginative contests to create a unique event, which the community can claim as its own and from which it capitalizes. But unlike throwing cow chips or beef tongues, digging postholes is more than a novelty. It is an athletic competition that takes some real brawn.

Oklahoma Panhandle State University wins Boise City's 2006 posthole digging contest.

RED CARPET COUNTRY

For three minutes, contestants try to dig the deepest posthole in the panhandle's parched pastures. With each hand wrapped around a pole and elbows raised above the shoulders, contestants slam the double-bladed shovel into the ground, then yank the poles apart, and lift out what little dirt their shovel will hold. This is done over and over until the muscle burn is unbearable, Carson says. At the end of three minutes, the deepest hole wins.

Carson says it didn't take much for the contest to gain some steam and become the showcase event during the celebration. Over the years it has drawn competitors from all of the lower forty-eight states, Carson said. The town also boasts that nobody has challenged Boise City's claim as home to the World Champion Posthole Digging contest.

Five years after the contest started, the volunteer Fire Department began hosting the event as its annual fund-raiser. Unfortunately, as popular as the event is, it hasn't raised any funds for the department. In fact, the city has to supplement the cost for holding the event. You see, the prize money for the different categories is far greater than the dollar entry fee. Sometimes digging yourself into a hole once a year for the sake of fun is worth it; at least Boise City folk think so.

The seven-day Santa Fe Trail Daze is held annually starting the last Tuesday of May. For more information on the celebration or posthole competition, call (580) 544-3479.

Lights Out
Boise City

Boise City, Oklahoma, holds a unique place in history. It's the only city in America to be bombed by an aircraft flying overhead during World War II. On July 5, 1943, at 12:30 a.m., the sleeping town was blasted with six one-hundred-pound bombs dropped by a B-17. The "attack" was a U.S. military training mission that had gone awry. Dalhart Army Air Base in Texas had ordered a hit on a site about 30 miles to the southeast of the small town. But that night a rookie navigator was called in to replace his experienced counterpart, who had fallen ill. So when the rookie saw the four lights around the Cimarron Courthouse in the middle of Boise City, he thought he had spotted the target. "Hit 'em," the young airman reportedly yelled, and the crew gave it their best shot.

Fortunately, their aim was off that night and nobody was killed, even though the aircraft circled several times in attempts to hit the target. The first bomb missed the courthouse and destroyed a dilapidated garage to the northwest that was about 40 feet from the U.S. Post Office. The second grazed the wall of the Baptist Church about 150 feet from the first hit. The third bomb hit Cimarron Avenue north of the courthouse leaving a crater about 2 feet wide and 4 feet deep. The fourth missile blasted a hole about 10 yards from the front door of a residence, just missing a large gasoline truck parked nearby, and the fifth bomb landed about 30 yards from another residence. The sixth bomb exploded between a residence and the overpass on Highway 64. The airmen didn't get a seventh chance to hit the target because Frank Garret, an electric company employee, hurried to the main frame and flipped the switch that plunged Boise City into darkness, ending the attack. The B-17 crew received a severe reprimand, and the townsfolk of Boise City calmed down from their chilling experience. It is said that following the event, a notice was posted at the air base stating: REMEMBER THE ALAMO, REMEMBER PEARL HARBOR, AND FOR LORD'S SAKE, REMEMBER BOISE CITY.

Ironasaurus
Boise City

Watching over the Cimarron Heritage Center Museum is an 18,000-pound, 65-foot-long, 35-foot-high, "Cimarronasaurus," called "Cimmy." It's an iron replica of the *Apatosaurus,* also known as a *Brontosaurus,* discovered in 1931 about 8 miles east of Kenton.

Cimmy, named by a Boise City elementary student, is the dream of local historian Norma Gene Young, who has been fascinated with the Jurassic finds excavated in Cimarron County.

Young always wanted a replica of an *Apatosaurus* that was the exact size of the one found. She was able to make that a reality through the sales of two books she authored: *Footsteps* and *The Tracks We Followed.* The life-size iron dinosaur was constructed by Joe Barrington of

Cimmy, the 18,000-pound iron Cimarronasaurus, sits outside the Cimarron Heritage Center Museum.

Throckmorton, Texas, and Young donated the sculpture to the museum, representing the museum's paleontology exhibit.

Besides the dinosaurs, the museum has a host of exhibits ranging from history of the 1930s Dust Bowl to the Santa Fe Trail. The museum is located at 1300 North Cimarron. For more information call (580) 544-3479.

Rock of Ages
Cimarron County

When merchant T. Potts carved his name into the side of a Dakota sandstone bluff just west of Boise City in 1826, chances are he didn't know what would follow, or did he? Perhaps he understood human nature and the lure of immortalizing your own name at a specific point in time on a traveled route. Whether he did or didn't, more than 300 people followed his lead and chiseled their names into the stone cliff that is about 40 feet tall and 700 feet long. Boise City townsfolk don't really care why the names are on the rock; they are just ecstatic that visitors flock to the area to see the historic site along the Santa Fe Trail.

The most popular name on Autograph Rock.

RED CARPET COUNTRY

Locals claim Autograph Rock, a certified site of the Santa Fe National Historic Trail, is the most visited place in the state. But then, they are including all of those people who have stopped at it since the trail opened in 1822. Currently, the site draws about two thousand visitors from March to November every year.

Autograph Rock was a well-known campsite along the Santa Fe Trail because of its proximity to Cold Springs, a year-round reliable water source. The vast majority of the carved names were left during the height of travel along the Santa Fe Trail in the mid- to late 1800s. The trail linked Santa Fe, New Mexico, to Independence, Missouri. The most popular name on the rock is F. B. Delgado, one of several merchants using the trail to freight goods. As tensions grew along the trail between the traders and the Kiowa and Comanche Indians, military troops started patrolling it. U.S. Army infantry solider S. Brown, who guarded the area, left his name on the rock.

One of several rocky areas along Cold Springs with autographs dating back to the 1800s.

These names, left more than a hundred years ago, stir the imagination about the adventurous pioneers who sought a new life in the untamed West and the merchants who braved the trail knowing their business success depended on their ability to retrieve and deliver quality goods. Then, out of nowhere, you are catapulted out of the era of wagon trains and into the era of station wagons. Who the heck is the "John Thrasher Family 1973"? It just goes to show you that the blank slate of history is always up for grabs.

Although Autograph Rock is located on private property, visitors can get permission to visit it through an appointment with the Cimarron Heritage Center Museum by calling (580) 544-3479.

One of the more vivid names of the more than 300 carved on Autograph Rock.

Santa Fe Trail? Can't Miss It.

Cimarron County

The Panhandle is relatively sparse with unobstructed views of the horizon in nearly every direction. It's unlikely that a motorist traveling the two-lane highway would miss any historical marker, especially those that have a state-issued approach sign alerting that a historical site is just ahead. Apparently, officials thought otherwise when marking the longest and oldest commercial highway across the Great Plains—the Santa Fe Trail, which crosses Highway 325 about halfway between Boise City and Kenton.

The site has a stately granite marker that complements the landscape, as most historic markers do in the state. But there is also this enormous metal sign with large bright red letters bearing the name, Santa Fe Trail. Along with that sign is one that notes Fort Nichols is

A few reminders to be on the lookout for this historic site.

located 7 miles to the south and several other horizontal signs about waist high, containing historical text about the trail.

Granted, the trail played a significant role by providing the first major trade link between the eastern United States and Mexico. It is even believed that Spanish explorer Francisco Vásquez de Coronado was one of the trail's earliest travelers in 1541. The trail provided a road for wagon traffic from 1820 to 1870. The gold rush in the 1840s increased that traffic. The trail was abandoned in 1880 with the extension of the railroad into Colorado.

It seems that the commercial aspect of this historic highway won't go unnoticed, at least by those motorists who travel these parts.

You Can Run but You Can't Hide
Cimarron County

It takes only a visit to the top of Robbers' Roost, a rock mesa overlooking the Cimarron Valley, to understand why Captain William Coe chose the site in the late 1860s as the headquarters for his notorious gang. The view stretches over the valley for miles into the neighboring states of New Mexico and Colorado. There was no better lookout for outlaws, whose lives depended on knowing the comings and goings in the lawless territory of the Panhandle called No Man's Land.

Now, nearly 150 years later, the view remains roughly unchanged. It is still used as a lookout by property owner Allan Griggs, but for more spiritual purposes than for survival. It's a place where you can often find Griggs drinking a late afternoon beer while soaking in the breathtaking views as the sun begins its descent. It's also the ideal nightspot for catching renegade stars shooting across the blackened sky. Griggs is eager to show the historic roost to visitors. As he puts it, Robbers' Roost represents an important piece of the Panhandle's history—"it defined life in No Man's Land."

Griggs acknowledges he doesn't know as much as he should about Coe and his gang of squatters, but the stories are so numerous who would? There are a handful of different stories alone on how Coe made his way from being an army captain for the Confederate army to the leader of the thirty-member Coe Gang. From there, the stories continue and it's hard to sort which are true and which are lore.

Griggs will tell you, however, that the gang didn't hide out on Robbers' Roost in solitude quietly waiting to execute the next heist. Within their rock fortress, equipped with 4-inch port-holes used to unload a barrage of bullets at unwanted visi-tors, were the amenities any gang needed to relax from their strenuous livelihood—whiskey, piano music, and plenty of women, Griggs said while grinning.

Griggs has the perfect lookout on Robbers' Roost.

According to historian Norma Gene Young, the Coe gang was hunted for years by the New Mexico and Colorado militaries. It took a military cannon to finally fracture the integrity of Robbers' Roost. Most of the gang, including Coe, got away unharmed. Despite military attempts to capture Coe, it was a woman who took him down. On this particular day, a military posse was looking for Coe, who had escaped again from Fort Lyons in Colorado. The posse stopped at the Emery Ranch, a place Coe had occasionally sought food and rest while traveling to or from the roost, but Coe was not there. Mrs. Emery's husband joined the posse and they headed to the roost. No sooner was the posse out of sight, when a haggard Coe showed up at the ranch. His intention was only to eat, but Mrs. Emery convinced him that he needed to rest to build his strength. While he slept in the bunkhouse, she sent her twelve-year-old boy after the posse. A few hours later, Coe was in custody, returned to Colorado, and executed. It's been reported, but not confirmed, that years later workmen excavating an area close to where Coe was hanged unearthed a skeleton that had its wrists handcuffed and ankles shackled.

The roost can be visited by appointment. Contact Griggs at (580) 261-7447 or stop by the Merc in nearby Kenton, which Griggs also owns.

RED CARPET COUNTRY

These Girls Rock!
Cimarron County

An old maid and three lonely sisters have been hanging around No Man's Land near the Black Mesa for as long as anyone can remember. Their stately presence is a part of the fabric of the far western edge of Cimarron County. There is rarely a motorist taveling along Highway 325 just east of Kenton who doesn't stop by to see them.

The gals are actually rock formations, sandstone layers that mushroom out of the landscape on either side of the highway. They are one of the most photographed sites in the area, dating back to before statehood.

Can you spot the old maid?

The Old Maid resembles a human profile. It's believed that her name comes from her single presence. The Three Sisters is a little harder to distinguish from the highway due to the growth of trees between the formations, but that doesn't stop tourists from snapping photos of it. Some photographs taken back in the early 1900s clearly show the sisters huddled together.

For more information on the exact location of the girls, contact the Black Mesa State Park at (580) 426-2222.

True Confession or False Pretense

Enid

House painter David George committed suicide at Enid's Grand Avenue Hotel in 1903 by ingesting poison. His death would have gone relatively unnoticed had it not been for his deathbed confession that he was assassin John Wilkes Booth. This announcement set in motion a whirlwind of bizarre events that still has conspiracy theorists convinced it's true.

Although Booth allegedly was shot against orders by Sgt. Boston Corbett in 1865 as he hid in a Virginia barn, there is a lot of mystery and rumor surrounding the identification of Booth's corpse that scholars still question today. Many believe Booth, a talented actor who favored Shakespeare, escaped from the barn and used his craft to successfully conceal his identity.

While versions of the legend vary slightly, the gist goes like this. George, who was not a very good house painter, had a remarkable likeness to Booth. He always had money, loved to drink, and often quoted Shakespeare. George was the exact age as Booth, and reportedly a medical affidavit states he also had a fractured leg above his right ankle, a scarred right eyebrow, and crushed right thumb. Booth supposedly had those same injuries, which he received jumping off the president's box at Ford's Theatre after assassinating Abraham Lincoln. Even handwriting samples of the two men obtained by the Enid newspaper a week after George died were concluded to have been written by the same man.

George's body was embalmed at the local funeral home housed in Penniman's Furniture store. It is said that his body was placed in a chair in the furniture store window for the public to view before a Memphis lawyer named Finis Bates arrived and purchased it. Bates took advantage of the publicity of George's deathbed confession and began displaying the mummified cadaver at many sideshows, including the 1904 St. Louis World's Fair. The mummy quickly grew a reputation of being jinxed, leaving Bates and other showmen who exhibited it financially ruined.

Newspaper and magazine articles over the years perpetuated the legend. According to the Oklahoma Historical Society, Enid resident Henry B. Bass, an authority on Booth and the legend, said he saw the mummy as a boy. He also reportedly discovered the strange coincidence that Sergeant Corbett, who supposedly killed Booth in Virginia, is buried in Enid. Nobody seems to know what happened to George. There's no telling where his body is, but there sure is a lot of telling about where his body's been.

Beefing Up the Prairie
Enid

As dawn breaks over Enid, silhouettes of cattle begin to appear across the southwest edge of Government Springs Park, a watering hole on the old Chisholm Trail. The sight can literally cause you to look twice. It has even been reported that on foggy mornings, drivers passing through on U.S. Highway 412 have veered their vehicles after being startled by what looks like a herd of longhorns coming near them.

The life-size black iron cutouts are the creation of Bob Klemme, a Chisholm Trail historian. Klemme, who is in his late seventies, said he wanted to depict a cattle drive, "you know, something that would catch your eye. Make you think about those days, tell a story."

Bob Klemme and his cattle.

The display does just that. On a two-acre area, there are twenty-four longhorns, six cowboys riding horses, a chuck wagon pulled by mules, and one Indian on a horse waiting for the cattle drive to reach a nearby creek. Buffalo grass was planted on that side of the park to bring more authenticity to it, Klemme said.

This project is an extension of Klemme's effort to mark the Chisholm Trail across Oklahoma. He is responsible for placing hundreds of 200-pound markers that are 6 inches square and 7 feet tall bearing the name CHISHOLM TRAIL, written in bold black vertical letters. He started marking the trial in 1990, but he's been studying the trail since he first learned about it in the ninth grade.

"It's a huge part of Oklahoma's history. I want young people to understand its importance. I thought showing a life-size cattle drive would have a better impact than just having a sign," he said.

There is no doubt that the cattle drive silhouette makes an impression. Government Springs Park is located on the southeastern side of Enid off US 412.

Rocky Start

Enid

Dan Midgley never turned down an opportunity to pick up an unusual stone or a truckload of the exotic mineral deposits, for that matter. Nearly every stone he has collected can be found inlaid in the walls or on display in his former home, the Midgley Museum in Enid. While people now flock to see the rock home and its contents, Midgley endured many a stony-faced neighbor, ridiculing him over his collection of materials for his dream home. As Midgley's quest for just the right rock grew, so did the pile of stones, fossils, and petrified wood that he stored on a vacant residential lot that he owned in an affluent neighborhood.

Watching the mound grow on the lot triggered several nearby residents to

Museum coordinator Joy Robertson stands in front of an unusually constructed fireplace.

voice their disapproval, both loudly and often. Midgley tolerated the harassment for a bit before holding a meeting and explaining that the rocks were going toward the construction of a spectacular home for him and his wife. He also warned those in attendance that if the badgering didn't stop, he would buy another lot in the area and build an eyesore. It's not clear whether the assurance or the threat put a stop to the harassment, but it stopped.

That's not the only run-in Midgley had over collecting rocks for his house. Midgley personally chose thirty-four different varieties of rocks for their color and texture. Unhappy with the lack of the color contrast in Oklahoma's petrified wood, he sent his workmen and a large truck to Arizona to collect the more colorful type. When the workmen returned with a truckload of the beautiful petrified wood, they also unknowingly brought along Arizona lawmen. Midgley was ordered to return the petrified wood and was fined twenty-five thousand dollars for taking it from the Petrified Forest National Park, protected reserve. There is a seven-thousand-pound petrified tree stump still displayed in the front yard, but Midgley claims it was found in Woodward.

The home was completed in 1947. By design or by accident, the house is acoustically perfect. There are also some surprising rocks built into the structure. There is a perfectly shaped seahorse protruding from the wall on the southeast corner of the house, and at the back porch there is a small green translucent rock that if you look closely you can see the name Dan Midgley and 1945.

Midgley and his wife, Libbie, lived in the home until their deaths, so the museum is filled with their belongings, ranging from rare china and antique appliances to an extensive exotic rock collection that includes a fluorescent mineral display. The Midgleys were expert hunters and skilled marksmen, and there is a trophy room, displaying many of their kills ranging from buffalo to a "freak caribou," which is a cross between a cow and caribou.

Today the museum is operated by the Northwestern Oklahoma Masonic lodges. It is open Wednesday through Friday. For hours of operation and group and special showings, call (580) 234-7265.

Seeing the Beauty from the Inside Out

Freedom

A group of young would-be spelunkers, wearing oversized hardhats and armed with flashlights, quietly wait as two adults prepare them for a self-guided, wild-caving adventure in the undeveloped grottos of Alabaster Caverns State Park south of Freedom. A visitor waiting for a guided tour spies the group of adolescents and decides to have some fun. He tells the children not to worry because nearly all who dare to venture underground without a ranger usually return safely.

"What happens to those who don't?" asks one apprehensive boy.

"Why the bats get them," the visitor replies.

A quick intervention by one of the adults cuts the conversation short.

"Thanks," says the group leader, who sounds annoyed. "That should make this trek a lot easier."

What the youngsters are about to enter is an underground wonderland that is one of only three in the world. The Alabaster Caverns State Park encompasses 200 acres beneath Woodward County, where the temperature drops to 50 degrees. It is home to the largest fine-grain gypsum caverns in the world that are designed for touring. These caverns are made of alabaster. Ninety-five percent of the other caverns in the world, including the famous Carlsbad Caverns in New Mexico, are made of limestone. The guided tour takes visitors over 330 steps through a three-quarter-mile long cave that contains massive alabaster boulders in pink, white, and a rare black color and glistening with selenite crystal formations, the result of 200 million years of nature's work. The area was once an inland sea, and when it slowly evaporated, huge deposits of gypsum formed and were carved out over time by roaring rivers. The caverns are also home to five species of bats. The park is one of the few that allows wild caving for anyone in five of its undeveloped caves from March through September, if spelunkers are properly equipped and permitted. For outdoor enthusiasts who shy away from subterranean treks, the park has four hiking trails.

Alabaster Caverns State Park is located on Highway 50A about 6 miles south of Freedom. It also has tent and RV camping sites. Daily cave tours are offered year-round. For more information on the fees, contact park rangers at (580) 621-3881 or visit www.tour oklahoma.com.

Naturalist Tandy Keenan exits the main cave at Alabaster Caverns.

Country Western
Freedom

Travelers passing through Freedom may think they have taken a wrong turn somewhere and have ended up on the set of an old Western movie. With nearly all of the building fronts made of weathered native cedar wood, the entire town looks like it came right out of the Wild West, with its Main Street primed for a shoot-out at high noon.

Freedom sits on the north banks of the Cimarron River just north of rugged canyons once occupied by Indians and then outlaws. From the beginning, this town has shown perseverance. The original town site is actually located about 5 miles north of its present location and was a thriving farming community. Merle Burkhart, director of the Freedom Museum, said that when the railroad linking two nearby towns was constructed in 1918, the Freedom townsfolk "just picked up their belongings and moved to here."

Burkhart says the town's population is about two hundred and fifty, "if you count the dogs and cats." But once a year on the third weekend in August, that population grows about twenty-five times during the annual Freedom Open Rodeo and Old Cowhand Reunion. The event includes everything from nightly rodeos and western dancing to country crafts and free, authentic chuck-wagon dining. The highlight of the event is a melodramatic reenactment of the "Great Freedom Bank Robbery and Shoot-out" by local residents.

The local museum houses memorabilia from the late 1800s to the early 1900s. There are also artifacts from the Burnham Dig, an archaeological site nearby where a mammoth sloth some thirty-five thousand years old was found, says Burkhart. For more information on the rodeo event or museum, call (580) 621-3583.

Salvage Art
Gage

The late Jim Powers left an artful mark not only in the small town of Gage, but also worldwide by sculpting unusual pieces out of junkyard scrap metal. Up until the day Powers died in the summer of 2006, he saw the beauty in the discarded metal waste that often becomes unsightly litter along the earth's rural landscape.

"Each time I use a bit of scrap, Mother Nature and Mother Earth seem to smile at me," he was quoted as saying in several publications.

Although much of his work is scattered across the world, some of his imaginative junk art is at the former Powers Salvage in Gage. The place isn't hard to find because you can't miss the big dinosaur made of automobile wheel rims as you pass through town.

Jim Powers stands next to one of his popular sculptures.

After retiring from the military, the Gage native opened and operated a salvage yard until government regulations forced his second retirement. It was about that time that Powers started getting interested in art, says his wife Beuhla. Powers had told many people that he was able to express himself through piecing together and reshaping the scraps of metal. He called his enormous metal sculptures "outsider art." By definition, Powers was definitely an untrained artist who worked in isolation, but his work never went unnoticed like much other outsider art. In fact, Powers had something far more powerful that he poured into his work—his life experience and storytelling abilities. His work caught the attention of Ripley's Believe It or Not! and it decided to features twenty pieces of his work in seven different countries, said Beuhla. There is also an elephant in Korea, a dinosaur in Taiwan, a praying mantis in the Philippines, and a buffalo in Denmark, she said. There are many more sculptures large and small throughout Oklahoma and in other states.

An elephant sits on the grounds of the Jim Powers Junkyard Museum in Gage.

"None of his works came out of a book; it all came from him and his good sense of humor. I think that is why it is still so appealing," she said.

People and animals inspired the majority of Power's artwork, which is evident when viewing his collection. He's most known for his Jimmy Bird sculptures found on nearly everything, including the hood of his pickup truck. Powers was a powerful artist whose presence will be missed, but whose spirit and humor will live on through his incredibly unusual "outsider art."

Much of Power's scrap metal art can be seen through a chain-linked fence without an appointment. For more information visit www .powersville.net.

Painting the Town
Gate

It's amazing what a little paint can do to liven things up. It turned this little whistle-stop community called Gate, population about a hundred, into what looks to be a thriving community of never-ending activity. As you drive through Gate, cut in half by U.S. Highway 64, it seems at first glance that folks are out and about conducting their business or shopping. But a closer look reveals that the Quaker preacher, window-shoppers, playing kids, and loafing men are actually life-size murals of this farming community back in the early 1900s. Now there aren't just a few murals here and there; they're everywhere throughout the entire town. Anything that can be painted is and depicts a scene of what life likely was in Gate back then.

Painting the town started as a project inspired by the September 11, 2001, terrorist attacks, says local artist Marilyn Shanhan.

"Everyone was in shock and saddened by the event. I just wanted to bring out a smile, make people happy. Celebrate life," said the sixty-five-year-old. She painted the first mural on the Avery Grocery and Panhandle Heritage Museum. Shanhan said the project mushroomed over night. Shanhan's endeavor with the assistance of Janis Yauk, a full-time nurse, has changed not only the outlook of the townsfolk, but of travelers passing through.

One mural features a Concord stagecoach hooked up to a team of four horses entering town. The deceased fathers of Shanhan and Yauk, who had never met each other, are sitting and chatting near a fence by Laurie's Café. Other murals feature a dairy farmer, who has brought a wagonload of milk to town, and a blacksmith working. These are just a few of the scenes.

Gate is now a place where travelers stop, no matter what day of the week.

"They get out of their cars, walk around and take lots of pictures, but most of all they smile and occasionally laugh. Mission accomplished," Shanhan says.

A mural along the side of a downtown building by local artist Marilyn Shanhan.

Two Heads Are Better than One?

Goodwell

Neither the unusual collection of arrowheads nor the first printing press to cross the Mississippi makes the everlasting impression that the encased Hereford calf does at the No Man's Land Museum in Goodwell, according to museum director Debbie Colsom.

"Most everyone that comes here is looking for the calf. It's not that unusual of a sight any more," Colsom said. "But we don't care why they come, as long as the come."

The museum has gained a lot of attention over the past sixty years with the display of the two-headed calf born in the spring of 1932. It lived only about two weeks, Colsom said. It died on the day the No Man's Land Museum opened in its original location in Sewell-Loofbourrow Hall on Oklahoma Panhandle State University campus in Goodwell.

A two-headed calf lures many visitors to the No Man's Land Museum.

The calf was preserved in a standing position and placed in a glass case for viewing. Most visitors, especially the children, quickly find it.

The museum is now located in its own building at 207 West Sewell Street. The museum, part of the No Man's Land Historical Society, was established in 1934 by preterritorial pioneers living throughout the Panhandle. The purpose was to provide historical information of the entire Panhandle. There are rooms devoted to the lives of ranchers and homesteaders and a large room displaying the tools and pottery used by the ancient Native Americans who inhabited the region. The museum also has a room dedicated to the geological and paleontological finds of the region.

One of the more unique items on display is a catlinite peace pipe given to a Hooker resident in 1923 by Blackfoot chief Two Guns Whitecalf. The chief's profile appears on the buffalo nickel.

The founders of this museum no doubt put their heads together when selecting the items for display. With or without the two-headed calf, a visit to the museum will provide a glimpse into the long ago lives of those who dared to settle in the untamed, lawless territory of No Man's Land. For information on museum hours, call the museum at (580) 349-2670.

A Crap Shoot

Hardesty

Cow manure was once considered a hot commodity—the brown gold of pioneer days coveted by settlers across the prairie. It not only heated up homes and cook stoves, but in one community, it ignited such a stink between two families that it ended with an ousting and two killings.

The feud started around 1884 when the Eldridge family settled a homestead in No Man's Land on the Beaver River near Old Hardesty. The Eldridge men started a cattle ranch, driving their herds from Cherokee Strip. Soon after, a family named Johnson staked a claim nearby. It didn't take long for the two families to recognize that each needed something from the other. The Eldridges wanted to cross the Johnsons' land to gain access to grazing fields, and the Johnsons wanted access to the river, which was on land owned by the Eldridges. So, an agreement was made—access to water for access to grazing. Everything was peaceful until the neighboring families began gathering cow chips for the approaching winter season.

The sun-dried manure patties were the heating source of choice back then, especially in the dead of winter. It burns odorless and sootless, with an intense heat beyond what a wood fire can provide. The Eldridges began collecting the manure from the Johnsons' land, claiming that the multitude of chips came from their cattle since the Johnsons owned only one dairy cow. The Johnsons disagreed and the historic feud was on. Soon after, the Eldridges cut off the water access to the Johnsons. This was followed by an Eldridge being shot at and some cattle being killed near the river. The Eldridges blamed the Johnsons. A gun battle soon ensued, and in the end an Eldridge boy was dead. Finally, the No Man's Land Vigilance Committee of Grand Valley ordered both families to leave the territory. The Eldridges moved across the border into Texas. The Johnsons eventually moved to the Cherokee

Strip, but on their way a sniper killed one of them. Although there was no proof, the Johnsons blamed the Eldridges.

Later, the Eldridge family was allowed to return to Old Hardesty after the committee was petitioned by area residents, who thought the unfair treatment of the Eldridge family was awful crappy. The family returned and operated the Eldridge Post Office until 1900.

The historic feud is documented at the No Man's Land Museum in Goodwell. The museum is located at 207 West Sewell Street. For more information call (405) 349-2670.

No Ordinary Fellows Here

Hooker

Folks around here know the Fischer boys aren't just any Tom, Dick, and Harry; they're the real thing. The three middle-aged brothers have spent their lives trying to convince people from outside this tiny town that they really are Tom, Dick, and Harry.

"People just don't want to believe it," Tom said.

In fact, their names got the brothers a pretty good deal on a mower after the salesman popped off that "not any ol' Tom, Dick and Harry could buy this particular mower." The salesman's pitch was to just Tom and Harry, who with their brother Dick operate Fischer Bros. farm. The two brothers informed the cocky salesman that he might have to eat a little crow because he was actually peddling his product to a Tom, Dick, and Harry. Of course, the salesman didn't believe them. So, a one-hundred-dollar bet was made and the brothers hollered for Dick. But, Dick's presence wasn't enough to convince the salesman, who insisted they show their driver's licenses as proof. In the end, the brothers bought the mower for a hundred dollars cheaper than the negotiated price. Tom said that was the only time their names actually worked to their advantage.

RED CARPET COUNTRY

A blessing or a curse, naming the only boys born into the Fischer family Tom, Dick, and Harry wasn't a long-time plan. It is the result of their great-grandmother's humor. You see, Dick is the oldest son. Then two years later came Tom. So, when the third child was expected, Dick said his great-grandmother "jokingly told our parents that if the next child was a boy, Dick and Tom definitely needed a Harry." And when the third baby turned out to be a boy, he was named Harry. When their mother became pregnant with the fourth child, great-grandma spoke up again as names were being considered.

"Every Tom, Dick and Harry needs a John," she quipped.

Thank goodness, the fourth child was a girl.

These guys are easy to find; either go to the Fischer Bros. Farm or ask anyone in town.

Brothers Tom, Dick, and Harry are farmers in Hooker.

Oklahoma CURIOSITIES

What's in a Name?

Hooker

Folks in this small town sure have a good sense of humor. You would, too, growing up in Hooker. Folks here decided a long time ago to embrace their town name and have a little fun with it. They named their American Legion baseball team, "Hooker Horny Toads," and during fund-raisers for the high school sports teams, they put up banners that said "Support your local Hookers." The Garden Club members proudly call themselves "Happy Hookers," and there is the Hooker Police Department, Hooker Lumber, and up until recently the Hooker Hardware.

Their spirited disposition of this town won them the Most Ridiculous Town Slogan Contest in 2005 with, "It's a location, not a vocation." Other popular mottos residents spout include, "All my friends are Hookers," and "I'm not your typical Hooker."

When asked how the town of about 1,780 residents got its name, some will tell you it was the surname of the military man who helped found the town. Others, however, say it came from the practice of hooking steer and leaving them for the railroad to collect.

Everything is Not So Crystal Clear beneath the Mud
Jet

Treasure hunting is only fun when you find what you're looking for. At the Great Salt Plains Park near Jet, finding the treasure is guaranteed, if you're willing to get dirty digging for it.

Beneath the vast expanse of exposed brown sand dusted with white salt and devoid of any vegetation lies the ever-forming dark chocolate selenite, a crystallized gypsum. Visitors come from across the country and around the world to hunt for the single crystals or the more popular large star-shaped clusters. This is the only location in the world where these crystals are found. On a dry day in areas where no digging is occurring, the light coating of salt blankets the brown sand resembling images of a lunar surface.

The area, 7 miles long and 3 miles wide, was formed millions of years ago when trapped sea water evaporated, resulting in large salt deposits, a mineral harvested by Indian tribes and early settlers. The crystallized gypsum is found just below the surface no deeper than about 2 feet. Bits of wet sand, soil, and clay are trapped within the crystal and often form the hourglass shape. But other debris in the soil like sticks, rocks, and even a misplaced cocklebur or two will find its way inside a crystal, park rangers say.

Great Salt Plains Park is open for crystal digging from April to mid-October. However, the novice digger, who wants to ensure finding treasure worth the effort, may want to come during the Crystal Festival held the last weekend of April or first weekend May. There are experienced selenite miners available to help guide your dig. A trip to the salt plains should include a diddy bag with shovel, a small container to splash water, a container to store crystals, sunscreen, and sunglasses, because the sun reflects off the salt. Also bring lots of water, both for drinking and washing off the crystals.

To find crystals, go to the designated digging area, dig a hole about 2 feet deep and in diameter. When the hole starts automatically filling with water, splash the sides to wash the soil away. Once you find a crystal formation, continue to splash water on it until it is free. The crystals are very fragile until they dry, so be careful. For more information on Great Salt Plains Park and the Crystal Festival, visit www.greatsaltplains.com or call (580) 596-3053.

Grab your shovel.

A Wonderful Bird Is the Pelican. His Bill Will Hold More Than his Belican.

Jet

The only pelicans normally seen in Oklahoma are the pink plastic ones dotting trailer parks and the front lawns of many rural residences. Some Okies might scratch their head when they learn about the seasonal white pelicans that flood the Great Salt Plains Wildlife Refuge every year in early September.

In celebration of the annual bird migration, the Great Salt Plains Association holds its Pelican Celebration, when thousands of pelicans stop over in the refuge to feed and rest on their journey from Canada to Texas and Louisiana for the winter. The population of the pouched-billed bird that lands in the refuge ranges between twenty and fifty thousand birds. The pelicans are 4- to 5-feet tall, have a wingspan of 8 feet, and feed primarily on the small carp and shad in the shallow Salt Plains Lake.

The pelicans can be watched at the lake spillway or Cottonwood Point on Highway 38. The areas are equipped with spotting scopes. While there, viewers may encounter a sea of other waterfowl, shore-birds, and even songbirds. The refuge is home to more than three hundred different bird species along with other wildlife. The American Bird Conservancy recognizes the area as a Western Hemisphere Shorebird Preserve.

I can't help but wonder what the northern white pelicans think of their pink plastic counterparts as they fly over the state. For more information on festival dates, hiking trails, or automobile routes through the refuge call (580) 596-3053.

It's the "Merc" That Marks This Spot

Kenton

It doesn't much matter which direction you're headed, whether you're entering Oklahoma's Panhandle driving east, or leaving it cruising west. The Kenton Mercantile, a rustic general store, is a stop everyone seems to make. Resting on the western edge of No Man's Land in the Black Mesa valley 2 miles from New Mexico and 7 miles from Colorado sits the town of Kenton with about thirty residents, a few churches, a tiny museum, the mercantile, and two gas pumps.

Allan Griggs mans the last stop entering or exiting Oklahoma's western edge.

It doesn't sound like much, but those who stop at the "Merc" get a lot more than expected.

Usually, it's gas, directions, or a cold drink and something to eat that lures the customer into the store, and there usually sitting behind the register or behind the grill they are greeted warmly by Allan Griggs, owner of the "Merc." The ex-engineer, who apparently has never met a stranger, spent years working for an oil company in the Middle East and speaks a couple of languages at least well enough to impress some foreigners stopping by. His place is the hub of activity for the town, which entails a few locals gathered to watch sports on the store TV. It's also the only joint in 35 miles where you can buy a meal, so his Beefosaurus Burger is a hot commodity.

The rickety store was built in 1898 by Drew Barnum, nephew of P. T. Barnum, a fitting founder considering the array of characters who live in town or stop by as they're traveling through. It has everything from toiletries to a wall of prehistoric fossils, which is the collection of the Kenton Mercantile Museum. And if you're up for some chitchat, Griggs is loaded with local gossip, politics, and general historical knowledge of Cimarron County. There never seems to be a lull in conversation.

He and his wife moved to Kenton in 1986 to create a burgundy vineyard in this semiarid landscape, specializing in pinot noir. While waiting for the vineyards to mature, his wife basically ran the store. Then she was diagnosed with cancer and the couple's efforts were focused on her health. She later died in 1998. The vineyard plan has yet to be successfully executed and is still on Griggs' list of things to do. Meanwhile, he's making small talk with visitors, mainly foreigners, and flipping burgers for whoever shows up hungry at lunchtime.

Griggs also owns three furnished, fully-equipped small cabins outside the store and the only gas pumps for 35 miles. For more information on renting a cabin, contact Griggs at (580) 261-7447.

Time Travel
Kenton

Kenton is the westernmost city in the state's panhandle and a place where you can manipulate time at its town limits. Unlike all of the other cities in the state, Kenton is the only one that chose to be on Mountain Standard Time, which technically starts 3 miles to the west at the New Mexico border. The rest of Oklahoma is on Central Standard Time. I couldn't find anyone around town that could tell me why that is although they boast that is just one advantage to living in the sleepy town.

So I guess it shouldn't be any surprise that the town also is considered to be one of the darkest spots in the state, which is an easier fact to figure out since there are no streetlights or yard lights, or highway lights for that matter. This is a town where its residents prefer to remain in the dark, an attraction that often draws stargazing clubs to the area.

Dino-Might
Kenton

Pard Collins made a discovery in 1931 of prehistoric proportions when the blade of his grader unearthed a bone off Highway 325 just east of Kenton. That one bone led to a find that is thought to be the largest *Apatosaurus,* formerly known as *Brontosaurus,* in existence—80 feet long, 40-feet tall and weighing in at 40 tons.

When paleontologist Dr. J. Willis Stovall was notified about the find, he swooped into the area, scooped out the dinosaur and several other specimens, and whisked them back to the University of Oklahoma. The *Brontosaurus* was fully reconstructed and is on display in the Oklahoma Museum of Natural History in Norman.

Not to worry, the scientist didn't want Kenton to feel as though it had been cheated out of its spectacular find. Kenton was thrown a bone—a life-size concrete replica of the *Apatosaurus'* femur measuring 5 feet, 11 inches in length. The real femur weighs about 425 pounds. The replica bone sits on top of a platform above the quarry next to the highway about 8 miles east of Kenton on the north edge of Highway 325. It is easily spotted from the road and has hundreds of tourist visiting the site annually.

The excavation of the site revealed 918 bones and teeth. More than thirty-six hundred perfect specimens were cataloged, and evidence was uncovered that indicated five different species of dinosaurs had died at the quarry site. Eventually, eighteen tons of bones were moved to the university.

Dinosaur tracks located in Cimarron County near the Black Mesa.

Finding Jurassic remnants in and around Kenton is not unusual and many of the residents have some pieces. There is even a series of dinosaur tracks embedded in the strata of solid rock in the bed of a creek on private land near the Black Mesa. Scientists believe the area was once a swamp and that the tracks are likely from plant-eating dinosaurs because of the large size and webbed toes. Except for the *Tyrannosaurus,* man-eating dinosaurs left smaller tracks and were pointy-toed.

These dinosaurs are estimated to be about 30 feet long and to have walked on hind legs, since no front prints are visible. There also are no tail tracks. The tracks are believed to be at least 150 million years old.

Each time it rains, the tracks fill with mud. Black Mesa State Park manager Ron Mills said he tries to keep them cleaned out because when people hear about them, they want to see them. These tracks, when cleaned out, still show how the weight of the dinosaur pushed the mud up to one side on each step. For directions to the tracks, contact Mills at (580) 426-2222 or ask any one of the thirty residents in Kenton.

Too Hot to Handle

Panhandle

There is a good reason why Oklahoma's Panhandle is called "No Man's Land." Some may think it's because of the lack of people. The population is so small that the 2000 U.S. Census Bureau classified it as frontier status, which is the most remote category indicating that there are six or fewer residents per square mile. But that's not the reason for its name. This strip of land, nearly 35 miles wide, 167 miles long, and bordered by four states, became known as No Man's Land because for a period of time it didn't belong to any territory or state. It was a lawless, untamed, orphaned region, whose inhabitants were left to fend for themselves.

No Man's Land.

The area had been a part of Texas territory, but when Texas established its borders in 1850, it relinquished that strip to protect its right to permit slavery. You see, any land north of the thirty-sixth parallel, which this area is, went with the Union and allowing slavery was doubtful. New Mexico set its borders the same year, then Kansas and Colorado followed, and when all the line drawing and deal making were complete, what was left unclaimed was this strip of land abutting all those states and Indian territories.

This unprotected strip quickly took on the name No Man's Land. It became a haven for outlaws, squatters, and cattle ranchers who made up their own rules for resolving disputes that usually involved six-shooters. It stayed that way for about forty years.

By 1887 a surge of immigrants who moved into Kansas and Colorado spilled over into the Panhandle, spiking its population to about six thousand. But nobody could legally claim land, be married, or establish a company. So, the people decided to organize and become their own territory. The effort was as wild and hostile as the region's reputation. It ignited much political posturing and meddling that some say ultimately killed any chance of it becoming a separate territory. Instead, No Man's Land was merged in 1890 with what had become Oklahoma Territory, creating the panhandle shape to the area. It became the seventh county seat, named Beaver, until statehood in 1907 when the Panhandle was divided into its current three counties of Cimarron, Texas, and Beaver.

No Man's Land is unlike any area of the state. The climate is semiarid and wide-open space is in abundance. A grocery store, stoplight, or neighbor can be miles away, if not located in the next county. Living in No Man's Land continues to be for the tough-hearted.

RED CARPET COUNTRY

The Pen Is Mightier than the Sword?

Perry

Just east of Perry there is a smattering of homemade billboards that resemble a giant ransom note with words and phrases pieced together in a rambling text about government corruption, conspiracy, and even murder. There is no missing this site if you're traveling Highway 64 between Perry and the Cimarron Turnpike. The majority of the signs line the highway much in the same way that the old Burma Shave advertisements once did. There are also large, square, black-and-yellow flags strategically placed throughout the property that can be seen from at least one-quarter mile away. It's unclear when the first of the thirty or so signs was erected on this rural farm, owned by a Czech family. Some of the signs look fairly new, while others are faded and difficult to read. Locals, who are willing to talk about the signs, say they remember them being there as far back as the mid-1970s.

For some people the barely comprehensible billboards are touted as a form of folk-art protest. On the Internet, the site has been called the X-Files ranch, perhaps because of references on some billboards to devil worshippers and witchcraft. But for David Nemechek, it appears the thirty-year-old display has been his only method to publicly retaliate against what he believes to be an injustice against his family at the hands of Noble County officials.

Words like *conspiracy, lies, murder, confess,* and *racism* and phrases like *We Are Whistleblowers* are highlighted in the rambling text. Even after reading the wordy and at times erratic text, it's difficult to discern what actually triggered all of this. Apparently in 1973, David and his wife, Mildred, began to encounter strange happenings at the farm. There was a drumming noise at night, harassing phone calls, farm equipment stolen, livestock mutilated, and crops poisoned. One sign goes as far as to say Mildred was murdered by "a mental torture

271

death," and a son was sent away. One sign implies the Nemecheks are victims of a Noble County white-supremacist cult that has ties with the sheriff, whose name is blacked out. They accuse the sheriff of failing to stop the persecution.

So many motorists have apparently stopped to look at the display, trying to figure out what the massive display means that the county had to erect signs prohibiting parking on the shoulder of the two-lane highway. There is a driveway available for parking and the Nemecheks have a small sign thanking people for stopping. There is no open access to the farmhouse. Some motorists who have stumbled across the signs have posted photos of them on the Internet. One person who posted photos noted that while he was viewing the farm, he was closely watched by lawmen.

Protest signs outside of Perry warn drivers of an alleged conspiracy.

RED CARPET COUNTRY

A check of court records show that in 1993 the sheriff won a libel lawsuit against the Nemecheks and had their property seized to satisfy the judgment. It's unclear why the protest display remains if the land was seized. The Nemechek family may have lost the battle with the law, but for the past thirty years, and who knows how much longer, their written protest will continue to live in Noble County.

Windy City
Shattuck

Dotted across Oklahoma's landscape are windmills turning in the prairie wind. There are old ones, new ones, broken ones, and even a few high-tech ones. But, there is no place in the state that has as many vintage windmills all in one spot as the Shattuck Windmill Museum and Park. The four-acre site is home to a collection of forty-five windmills, dating from the late 1800s to the mid-1900s.

Windmills were the principal energy source that made possible the settlement of the Great Plains. Pioneers used the wind-powered devices to pull water from underground aquifers. Shattuck residents are banking on the prairie wind to blow tourists in to see the vintage collection that made homesteading possible.

The collection, which is thought to be the fifth largest in the country, is made up of a variety of brands and sizes. The Eclipse, one of the earliest windmills, has a fan that tilts upward to catch the light breezes. The Hummer has a cast-iron chicken for counterbalance, and the Challenge has twin tails. Older windmills have wooden towers, and windmills made of factory-produced steel came in the early 1900s. They were made with either three or four legs.

Shattuck is part of the American Wind Power Trail, a partnership between Oklahoma and Texas designed to use windmills, weather, and wind energy to help tourists to understand the history of the Great Plains. Shattuck's museum is a stop along the American Wind Power Trail.

These wind machines have brought a whirlwind of tourism to this sleepy, windswept little town since the museum opened in 1996.

The collection is located on a field at Highways 283 and 15. For more information call (580) 938-2818.

A collection of vintage windmills dates from the late 1800s to the mid-1900s.

RED CARPET COUNTRY

"Let's Play Twister!"
Wakita

This quiet farming community of Wakita was temporarily jolted out of an economic slumber in 1995 when it experienced its only tornado ever—compliments of Hollywood. Oklahoma's location in the heart of "Tornado Alley" piqued the interest of Hollywood producers, who were searching for a place to shoot their big-budget disaster film, *Twister,* and out of all the potential sites, Wakita got top billing.

It seemed funny to some townsfolk that Wakita, population a little more than four hundred, would be selected, since tornadoes didn't seem to bother the town like they did other communities and big cities. The closest any tornado has gotten to Wakita was in March 1990, when an F3 tornado hit 8 miles northeast of the town.

"I can't remember the last time a tornado hit here. We can sometimes see them forming way out there as they turn and head north toward Kansas," said seventy-eight-year-old Jeraldine Evans, a Wakita resident and manager of the city's Twister Museum, the only tornado museum in the state.

The museum, however, gets all of its twister displays from the fictional movie. Among the leftover movie props donated to the museum by Warner Bros. is "Dorothy I," a totable tornado observatory. There are also a multitude of candid photographs, depicting the making of the movie from start to finish, and of course autographed photos from the actors and costars, Bill Paxton and Helen Hunt. Also on display is a segment of the old Loop House, which was refurbished for the movie to be the home of "Aunt Meg."

One of the main reasons the town was selected as the site for filming the movie was because it had sought a state grant to raze a host of abandoned buildings, which, of course, would produce rubble—talk about killing two birds with one stone. The film's wrecking crews came in and demolished the buildings, and the debris from the demolition was used to depict the aftermath of the tornado's wrath. The destruction was so convincing that a helicopter that happened to fly overhead stopped to investigate.

During filming, business boomed in Wakita, Enid, and Ponca City. Profits were made in the hospitality industry and on goods ranging from T-shirts to special food items, like the twister sandwich.

Wakita is the only town in the state to have tourists come to see the twister that wasn't really a twister at all. The museum is located at 101 West Main Street. For more information visit www.twister country.com.

Jeraldine Evans stands beside a totable tornado observatory used in the movie Twister.

TORNADO FACTS:

- The costliest tornado was an F5, measuring one-half to three-quarters of a mile in diameter, which made a swath through Oklahoma City, Bridge Creek, Moore, and Del City in May 1999, causing $1 billion in damage.

- The deadliest tornado was an F5 that hit Woodward in April 1947, resulting in 116 fatalities.

- There have been a dozen F5 tornadoes recorded in Oklahoma from 1905 to 1999.

- No tornadoes were reported in May 2005, the first time no tornadoes were recorded in the month of May since official records began in 1950. May is historically the most active month for tornadoes. The most ever recorded were ninety in 1999.

- Caddo County had a total of ninety-six tornadoes from 1950 to 2004, more than any other county in the state. Oklahoma County comes in second with ninety tornadoes. Adair County comes in last with thirteen.

Source: National Weather Service Forecast Office, Norman, Oklahoma

Say Cheese
Watonga

Watongans proudly admit they're cheesy people whey out there. Without shame, they have been publicly cutting cheese for nearly sixty years—cheddar cheese, that is. Since 1940, the Watonga Cheese Factory has been producing thousands of pounds of cheese from whole milk produced in Oklahoma. It now claims to be not only the oldest cheese factory in the state, but also the only one that specializes in cheddar. That hasn't always been the case. In the late 1940s, there were nearly thirty similar cheese factories, each buying their milk within a 25 to 40 mile radius. Cooling technology and growth in transportation capabilities,

Cheddar cheese for sale at the Watonga Cheese Factory.

however, decreased the necessity for small cheese factories and many closed down. Lucky for Watonga, its product never soured; it just aged to perfection.

The Watonga Cheese Factory was started by some local dairy farmers looking for a way to make money from their whole milk. They were able to sell their cream but had no place to sell the leftover skim milk that had been separated out. The farmers banded together and as a group agreed to buy a lot near downtown, convert a portion of an existing ice plant into what is now known as the Watonga Cheese Factory, and make cheese from their milk. The factory met the farmers' needs then and it continues to help the town today. Watonga has the distinction of being home to the only cheddar-cheese factory in the state. The factory produces a host of flavored cheddar from blocks to the popular bags of curds, and ranging in flavor from several-year-old aged cheese to firehouse for those who like a little heated cheese.

Twice a week, cheese is churned out in 10,000-pound loads, and once a year on the second weekend in October, the factory is open to the public during the Watonga Cheese Festival to demonstrate how the cheese is made.

The small plant takes Oklahoma milk, pasteurizes it, and puts it in a couple of long vats, where a few employees work it by hand before it is molded, packaged, and put on the shelves at the plant's tiny store and in supermarkets across the state.

Cheese can also be purchased online during the fall, winter, and spring. The plant's Web site is www.watonga.com. For information about the cheese festival, contact the Watonga Chamber of Commerce at (580) 623-5452.

INDEX

INDEX

INDEX

INDEX

INDEX

INDEX

About the Author

PJ Lassek is an adventurer at heart who is always up for the challenge, whether it's cycling across Ireland or spelunking with friends in unguided caves in Arkansas. Her quest in life is to experience as much as possible and still live to tell about it. She characterizes almost every unpredictable event that comes her way whether good or bad as only added color to what otherwise would be a boring black and white canvas of life.

She makes her living as a journalist for the *Tulsa World* newspaper. Although she currently reports on the serious side of news events within the arena of local politics, outside of her news writing she rarely takes on a serious demeanor, always searching for that smile or hearty laugh. So when approached to do this assignment, she definitely was intrigued. While she has freelanced for a few state, national, and international magazines during her more than twenty-year reporting career, this is her first attempt at writing anything longer than a thirty-inch story, let alone a book. PJ also is a cartoonist, which she says is more of a hobby than a business even though she has sold her work.

A native of Detroit, she was raised mostly in Oklahoma. She lived about five years in Los Angeles as a young adult before returning to Tulsa, where she lives with her dogs, Idgie Threadgoode, a fourteen-year-old Border Collie, and Guinness Smooth-n-Stout, a two-year-old Australian Shepherd.